Andrew Moss

True Crime Library
A Forum Press Book
by the Paperback Division of
Forum Design,
PO Box 158, London SE20 7QA

An Imprint of True Crime Library

Design and typeset by Ben James
Printed and bound in Great Britain by
Cox & Wyman, Reading, Berkshire

ISBN 1 874358 38 9

TRUE CRIME LIBRARY

LOVE YOU TO DEATH
A DATE WITH THE HANGMAN
BEDSIDE BOOK OF MURDER
FATAL ATTRACTION
STRANGE TALES FROM STRANGEWAYS
ON DEATH ROW
WOMEN ON DEATH ROW
MURDER WITH VENOM
A NEW CENTURY OF SEX KILLERS
BRITAIN'S GODFATHER
DIARY OF A HANGMAN
FROM WALL STREET TO NEWGATE
CAMINDA THE CRIME BUSTER
FROM THE X FILES OF MURDER
FAR FROM THE LAND
THE CORPSE GARDEN
THE BOOTLEGGERS
CLASSIC MURDERS OF THE NORTH EAST
(Magazine size 92 page edition)
CLASSIC MURDERS OF THE NORTH WEST
MURDER ONE
WOMEN WHO KILL VICIOUSLY
FORENSIC CASEBOOK OF CRIME
TONY MARTIN AND THE BLEAK HOUSE TRAGEDY

INTRODUCTION

There are many famous stories of murder, passion, intrigue, blood and gore. But are they just legends, or are they really true? And if they're true, did they really happen the way people tell it?

Did an immigrant German carpenter kill the young son of Charles Lindbergh, America's great hero? Or could the murderer have been Lindbergh himself? Did Lizzie Borden use an axe to "give her mother forty whacks," and her father another forty-one? Or was it, as she protested, an unseen intruder?

Was there a real-life Hound of the Baskervilles? Were all the Marquis de Sade's incredible sexual exploits for real, or just a figment of his imagination? Did Sweeney Todd really turn his victims into meat pies?

Such stories, which have baffled people for decades, always present several different theories, different findings, different answers. In this book 20 celebrated stories, all with a mystery murder or crime background, are examined in the light of new evidence to determine what really happened.

When you have read each one it will be for you to decide: was it murder, was it myth, or was it all just make-believe?

CONTENTS

1

CHARLES LINDBERGH

A slightly stained hero

By the time he was 25 Charles Lindbergh had done it all. He was a national hero and a living legend, fêted all round the world. After that everything in his world began to go downhill, and on the way some remarkably unheroic things happened.

Even so, the handsome, 6 ft 3 in stunt pilot had written his name in the record books with an achievement that was indelible. His lone flight across the Atlantic in 1927 established him as the winner of a $25,000 prize to become the first man to cross that ocean from New York to Paris in a heavier-than air machine.

The prize had been on offer since the end of the First World War, and several experienced aviators had died in pursuit of it. There had been the famous Alcock and Brown flight from Newfoundland to Ireland in 1919, but that covered 1,960 miles, whereas New York to Paris was 3,610 miles.

Despite the history of crashes and fatalities dogging the prize, Lindbergh was determined to win it. Not many who knew him gave him much hope. He had so far earned his living as a daredevil stunt man at air shows – this after only eight hours flying instruction in which he was not even given the chance to fly solo – and as a pilot carrying mail between mid-West cities for a private company.

His aircraft, *The Spirit of St. Louis*, largely designed by Lindbergh himself, was a shoestring affair compared with rival planes backed by major sponsors. It had no radio, no parachute, no forward view and its seat was a wicker basket chair to save weight. Lindbergh looked certain to add his name to the obituary list when he took off from New York at 0752 on May 27th. But thirty-three and a half hours later *The Spirit of St. Louis* touched down safely in Paris.

Everything had gone according to his carefully estimated flight plan. But in his single-minded concentration on his goal, there was one thing he failed to take into account. He didn't anticipate that his achievement would make him famous.

America's response to this young man's conquest of the Atlantic was overwhelming. President Calvin Coolidge sent a cruiser to bring him back from France, and of the 55,000 congratulatory telegrams he received one contained 17,500 signatures and had to be delivered in a scroll 520 feet long, carried by ten messenger boys.

After his triumphal ticker-tape welcome in New York, the Street Cleaning Department picked up 1,800 tons of paper, twelve times as much as after the Armistice celebrations nine years previously.

Lindbergh, however, was a reluctant hero. All this adulation and publicity shocked and embarrassed him. Overnight, the pilot employed by a small St. Louis airline had become an international celebrity.

He had also become wealthy and his projection into the ranks of the rich and famous brought him into contact with Dwight Morrow, the American ambassador to Mexico. Within months Lindbergh courted and married Morrow's daughter Anne.

Throughout the 1930s Lindbergh developed a passionate interest in Hitler's Germany. After several visits to Germany he reported back to America that the Nazis were invincible. When war broke out he spoke out virulently against American aid for Britain, and his popularity plummeted. In December, 1941, America entered the war and from that moment he served his country well, flying fighter planes against the Japanese as a sort of combat test pilot.

But the event that was to blight Lindbergh's life happened years earlier, when his baby son was kidnapped. Thousands of congratulatory telegrams poured in from all over the world when in 1930 the Lindberghs became parents of their first child, Charlie. Police were later to say that this ecstatic response to the great hero's new role in life captured the interest of would-be kidnappers.

At that time the Lindberghs' routine was to spend Mondays to Fridays at the Morrows' family home in New Jersey, moving on at weekends to the house Lindbergh had built near Hopewell, in the state's Sourland Mountains.

Unusually, they were at their Hopewell retreat on Tuesday, March 1st, 1932. They normally returned to the Morrows' home on Monday afternoons, but Lindbergh decided to extend their stay because Charlie had developed a cold. A strict disciplinarian, Lindbergh insisted that the baby was not to be spoiled and should be left alone from 7.50 p.m. when he was put to bed until 10 p.m. when he was toileted.

At ten o'clock the couple's Scottish nurse, Betty Gow, went to see Charlie as usual. His cot was empty. She hurried downstairs, thinking he must be with his parents. He was not with his mother, so the nurse went to the study where Lindbergh sat writing.

"Have you got the baby?" she asked. "Please don't fool me."

"What do you mean?"

"He's not in his crib or with his mother."

All three rushed upstairs to the nursery.

"Anne," said Lindbergh calmly, "they have stolen our baby."

Ordering the butler, Ollie Whately, to phone the police, Lindbergh went outside with a rifle and a torch while his wife and the nurse searched the house. Having called the police, Whately went out to Lindbergh's car and drove with him up and down the drive, shining a spotlight on both sides. Finding nothing, they returned to the house and Lindbergh went back to the nursery, calling attention to an envelope that lay on the window sill.

"Don't anyone touch that," he told his wife and the nurse.

"But it must be from the kidnappers," Anne protested. "Let's open it. It may tell us something important."

"No, we must wait until the police come," Lindbergh told her firmly. "It may have fingerprints."

When the officers arrived, clearly in awe of the tall, handsome hero, Lindbergh took command of the situation, indicating the envelope on the nursery window sill and clay on the floor between the cot and the window.

Examining the scene outside, the police found footprints leading from beneath the nursery window to bushes where they discovered a crudely-made extending ladder. Its rungs were 19 inches apart, so it was suitable only for a tall person, and the top rail was broken.

State troopers arrived to augment the local police, and the envelope was opened by a fingerprint technician. A note inside, crudely and laboriously written, said that the baby had been kidnapped and demanded a $50,000 ransom. The letter also told Lindbergh that he would hear from the kidnappers again soon, and warned him not to notify the police if he valued the baby's life. It was "signed" by an oval within three interlocking circles, each with a hole punched in the middle.

No fingerprints were found on the note, and it had apparently been written by a poorly-educated German. There were no fingerprints in the nursery either, or on the ladder.

"Our objective must be to get Charlie back alive and well," Lindbergh told the police. "We will meet the kidnappers' demand. Until the child is back with us, we ask you to stay out of the case. Nothing must be done that might frighten the criminals into harming the child."

The police agreed to this, but a hunt for Charlie was launched, nevertheless, and Ollie Whately, his wife – who was the Lindberghs' cook – and the nurse were questioned intensively. Detectives suspected that the kidnapping was an inside job. After all, who else would know of the family's last-minute change in their normal routine that had prompted them to stay at their Hopewell home longer than usual? And who else would be aware that Charlie was left untended from 7.50 until 10 every evening?

Lindbergh said he would seek the help of the New York underworld, and he was put in touch with Mickey Rosner, a conman, and the racketeer Owney Madden, giving them a copy of the ransom note.

A second note arrived two days later, raising the ransom to $70,000 because Lindbergh had informed the police. This and subsequent notes could have been forgeries made by anyone who had seen the copy of the original, but a police handwriting expert believed them to be genuine.

Al Capone, behind bars for tax evasion, announced: "If the government will let me out of here for ten days, I'll bring that baby back. I've got connections and I can find the kid." The authorities were unimpressed and his offer was not taken up.

In another development, Dr. John Condon, a 72-year-old retired schoolteacher, came forward to announce that he would add $1,000 to the ransom and would be pleased to act as an intermediary. He made his approach to a New York newspaper which duly reported his offer, and the next day he received a letter posted in Brooklyn and signed with the kidnappers' three-ring symbol. It welcomed Condon as an acceptable go-between and asked him to reply by placing an advertisement in the *New York American*.

Condon hurried to Hopewell and showed the note to Lindbergh, who summoned the police handwriting expert. It was decided that the letter was genuine, and Lindbergh asked Condon to act as his intermediary and reply to the kidnappers.

"Let them know I can have the money for them," he said. "Then we can arrange how the child is to be returned."

Meanwhile, Mrs. Evalyn McLean, a wealthy acquaintance of the Lindberghs, had independently approached

Gaston Means, a shady character who she believed had underworld contacts. Means told her he thought he knew who had kidnapped the baby, and he could soon find out for sure. He later reported back to her that he had confirmed his suspicion and now knew where the child was being held. But the kidnappers, he said, had increased their demand to $100,000. If they didn't get it quickly they might think the police were getting too involved and "destroy the evidence."

"You mean the baby?" asked Mrs. McLean.

Means nodded.

Mrs. McLean raised the money and gave it to him to give to the kidnappers. He reported that he had made the delivery, and the baby would be taken to Mrs. McLean's summer home in the Maryland hills. With two of her servants she went there to await the child's arrival.

Condon was equally busy. Further notes came and then a phone call from a man with a German accent who spoke about the ransom and said Condon would hear from him again soon. A baby's sleeping suit had meanwhile been sent to Lindbergh to establish the kidnappers' credibility. He thought it was Charlie's but could not be positive.

The next note instructed Condon to take the money with him at midnight that night and look under a stone outside a certain flower shop in New York's Bronx district. There he would find another note telling him where to take the cash.

Condon promptly phoned Lindbergh, who joined him in New York. Collecting $70,000 from a bank, Lindbergh stuffed it into a wooden box and two brown paper parcels. The notes' numbers had already been recorded, and $20,000 was in gold certificates which were no longer issued but were still valid currency.

Lindbergh then drove Condon to the flower shop. A note under the stone told the go-between to walk to a nearby cemetery. Arriving at the gate, he saw a man inside wave a white handkerchief. Condon approached him, but was unable to see his face in the darkness. The man held an envelope which he said contained details of where and when Charlie would be delivered. But before he handed it over, he wanted the money.

"It's in the car," Condon told him, indicating where the car, with Lindbergh sitting at the wheel, was parked, 80 yards away. Lindbergh was afterwards to recall that he heard the man call out, "Hey, Doctor!" to Condon.

"Go and get it," the man ordered.

Condon walked back to the car, collected the ransom, went and handed it over, and returned to the car with the envelope.

Eagerly, Lindbergh tore it open. Inside was a note saying that Charlie was on a boat called *Nelly*, moored off Martha's Vineyard, Massachusetts.

A two-day air and sea search failed to find any vessel called *Nelly*, and 72 days after Charlie's disappearance his decomposing body, without its sleeping suit, was found in a wood three miles from his home. At Lindbergh's request there was no post-mortem, and the remains were cremated.

In the aftermath Gaston Means was jailed for swindling Mrs. McLean. Anne Lindbergh gave birth to a second son, and the couple set off together to survey new routes for the airline Pan American.

In due time some of the ransom notes began to surface in the Bronx, but the police were unable to trace who was passing them. Then, on September 15th, 1934, one of the $10 gold certificates was used at a filling station to pay for petrol.

"You don't see many of these any more," said the pump attendant.

"I've still got about a hundred," the motorist told him.

To ensure he didn't get stuck with the certificate if the bank wouldn't accept it, the attendant wrote the customer's car number on the back of it. Two days later New York's Corn Exchange Bank identified the certificate as part of the ransom money. The police were called, the certificate was known to have been paid in by the filling station, and the attendant pointed out the car number he had noted.

The car was registered to Bruno Richard Hauptmann, a 34-year-old German carpenter living in the Bronx with his wife and infant son. When the police went to his home and arrested him, they found more than $14,000 of the ransom hidden in his garage.

Asked to account for this, he claimed he had found the money in a shoebox left in his safe keeping by an associate, Isadore Fisch, who had returned to Germany where he had since died. Fisch had been a fence who sold "hot" money at a discount, and Hauptmann said he had no idea where this particular cache had come from. He had simply concealed it in his garage for security, and had begun using it after he heard about Fisch's death. To support his story, he produced a book which had Fisch's name on the fly leaf.

His own history was chequered. Convicted of burglary in Germany, Hauptmann has arrived in America as a stowaway. He was now charged with kidnapping and murder, and he went on trial in New Jersey in January, 1935.

According to the prosecution, he had made the ladder found at the Lindberghs' home. One of its rungs was part of a floorboard from Hauptmann's attic. Driving to Hopewell, he had placed the ladder beside Charlie Lindbergh's nursery window, the only one at the house with an unlatched shutter.

Climbing into the room, he had taken Charlie from his cot, put him in a sack, left the ransom note, and was beginning to descend the ladder when a rung broke. This had caused him to drop Charlie, fracturing his skull. Discovering that the child was dead, he had hidden the ladder, put the body in his car and dumped it in the wood. Then he had returned to New York to write further ransom notes. Detectives had even found Condon's phone number written on the wall of a cupboard at Hauptmann's home.

It seemed like a copper-bottomed case, but it wasn't quite like that. First, the court was not told that a newspaper reporter had told colleagues how he himself had written Condon's number on the wall and had then called detectives' attention to it so that he could get the lead story the next day in his paper. Nor was the court told about the dubious background to the testimony of three poverty-stricken witnesses who claimed they had seen Hauptmann near the Lindberghs' Hopewell home at the time of the baby's disappearance. Determined to secure a conviction, the police had promised the trio cash for their evidence. The President of the United States had demanded that the kidnappers be caught, and the authorities had been criticised for their failure to deliver.

Lindbergh claimed in court that the voice he heard call "Hey, Doctor!" was Hauptmann's. Handwriting experts testified that the ransom notes appeared to have been written by Hauptmann, but their comparisons were not with the original note, but with the subsequent letters, which could be forgeries. A blind eye was turned to the fact that the ladder rung said to have been fashioned from Hauptmann's floorboard was thicker than those in his attic. And the crude ladder was obviously not the work of a carpenter.

Awkwardly for the police and the prosecution, Hauptmann had a sound alibi. His foreman had signed an affidavit confirming that the German carpenter was at his work until 5 p.m. on the day of the kidnapping, and the witness produced a signed time-sheet to prove it. This meant that Hauptmann could not have got to Hopewell in time to snatch the baby. The foreman had since withdrawn his statement and the police had somehow "lost" the important time-sheet.

Hauptmann could understand English only with difficulty, but he was not provided with an interpreter. His defence lawyer, hired by a newspaper, was an alcoholic incompetent who idolised Lindbergh, and the judge's summing-up was more like a speech for the prosecution than a neutral résumé of the evidence.

Bruno Richard Hauptmann was duly convicted and on

April 3rd, 1936, he went to the electric chair.

But was he guilty? And if he wasn't, who killed the Lindberghs' baby? At the time of his trial, no one bothered too much about whether Hauptmann was framed, and 50 years passed before the journalist Ludovic Kennedy published a book demolishing the prosecution's evidence. This was followed eight years later by a study of the case by two American experts in criminology, defence lawyer Gregory Ahlgren and police chief Stephen Monier. In court they were often adversaries, but in their book they jointly concluded that Hauptmann was innocent. And they came up with a plausible scenario for what they suggested really happened on the night of March 1st, 1932.

Their starting-point was something that had always puzzled the police. How did the kidnapper know of the Lindberghs' last-minute change in their arrangements, which led to their being at Hopewell when they would normally have been at Mrs. Lindbergh's parents' home? How did he know that the shutters of the nursery bedroom were the only ones at the house that wouldn't latch? And how did he summon the nerve to snatch the baby when people in the house were still up, lights were on and there was a dog which might be expected to bark?

It is small wonder that the police initially suspected an inside job. Ahlgren and Monier not only suspected it – they were convinced of it.

Lindbergh was never under police suspicion, but Ahlgren and Monier took a less blinkered view of the great hero. Researching his history, they learned that he was a control freak. His iron self-discipline and the precision he applied to everything helped to explain his pioneering solo flight across the Atlantic with just five sandwiches for sustenance. But even control freaks need breaks, and Lindbergh's form of release from his own tight self-control came in the form of callous practical jokes.

Once he put a fellow-pilot in hospital by lacing his drinking water with kerosene. At a party he embarrassed and incensed his wife by dribbling water down the back of her dress. And two months before Charlie's disappearance he told her that the baby had been stolen. He had hidden Charlie in a cupboard, so when the baby vanished for real his wife and the nurse at first thought this was another of Lindbergh's japes. That was why Betty Gow, finding the cot empty, begged Lindbergh, "Please don't fool me."

So was the kidnapping a practical joke that went horribly wrong? Did Lindbergh plan to carry Charlie down the ladder and then appear at the front door asking what the baby was doing in the garden? And did the joke turn to tragedy when the ladder-rung broke, causing him to drop Charlie?

Then, unable to face the ignominy of having accidentally killed his own son, let alone having to confess to his wife, did Lindbergh proceed to fake the kidnapping?

He had been in New York that day on airline business, and he did not arrive home until 8.25 p.m., half an hour later than usual. But his wife thought she heard a car outside at 8.10 p.m. Was it Lindbergh's? Instead of entering the house as usual, did he decide to play his joke on Anne, and when it went wrong, did he drive off to dump the body, honking his horn on his return 15 minutes later to ensure that everyone knew he was just back home?

What was he writing in his study? Was it the ransom note which neither the nurse nor his wife spotted until he drew it to their attention? Just before this he was alone in the nursery, with time to plant the envelope on the window sill.

A scenario with Lindbergh as the kidnapper resolves many otherwise unanswered questions. It explains how the kidnapping happened when it did, why the dog didn't bark, the baby didn't cry, and Mrs. Lindbergh and the nurse didn't notice the envelope beside the window upon which all eyes must have focused.

Charles Lindbergh is no longer around to confirm or deny this speculative account of what happened. He died in 1974. His widow, now in her nineties, never saw him shed a single tear over Charlie's fate. But then, he was a control freak.

As for Bruno Hauptmann ... he rejected an offer by the authorities to remit the death sentence in return for a confession. And he turned down a newspaper's offer to give his destitute widow $90,000 if he owned up. These were hardly the responses of a man who was guilty.

2

WILLIAM WALLACE

Not quite checkmate

Who was Qualtrough? If you know anyone who has ever met him, advise them to go at once to the police. Or did Qualtrough simply not exist? Was he just a figment of someone's imagination?

Qualtrough may have been the man who killed Julia Wallace, and if ever a murder were destined to become legendary, it was that of Julia Wallace. Nine writers subsequently turned the story into novels – dressing up a real-life drama as fiction.

None could eclipse the enigma that inspired them – a murder mystery which Raymond Chandler said would "always be unbeatable."

William Herbert Wallace, the diffident, mild-mannered husband of Julia, first heard about Qualtrough when he went for his usual game of chess at Central Liverpool Chess Club on January 18th, 1931.

As he was about to sit down the club captain, Samuel Beattie, said to him: "A Mr. Qualtrough phoned for you – R. M. Qualtrough. He said he's sorry he can't call back tonight because he's going to be busy making the final arrangements for his daughter's twenty-first birthday party. But he said if you care to meet him at 7.30 tomorrow evening at 25 Menlove Gardens East, he will pass on some business to you."

There was nothing unusual about such a message.

Wallace was area salesman for the Prudential Assurance Company – he was accustomed to doing business with strangers. Mr. Qualtrough, he thought, was looking for a policy, perhaps.

Beattie commented: "I must say, although I live in Menlove Avenue, Mossley Hill, I don't know where Menlove Gardens East is."

"Nor me," said Wallace. "But I'll find it. I can always ask if I get into trouble."

Straight after the chess game, Wallace went home to his rented terraced house at 29 Wolverton Street, Anfield. There he found his wife Julia upset about her cat, which had disappeared.

"I'm sure I'll never see him again," she said tearfully.

She was a tall, dark-haired woman with a somewhat distant manner, which tended to conceal her shyness. The Wallaces had once lived in Harrogate, and Julia still wasn't happily settled in Anfield, which she regarded as a bit of a come-down after life in the sedate spa town.

But she was trying to make the most of it. She played the piano well and held concerts in her front parlour, with her husband accompanying her, rather badly, on the violin.

In 1931 Wallace was 52 and for more than 15 years he had been a familiar, six-foot-two figure in the Clubmoor district of Liverpool, going from door to door as "the man from the Pru." They were a childless couple and had never been known to quarrel. They were also somewhat intellectual. Besides playing the piano Julia spoke fluent French, while her husband had turned the back bedroom of their house into a laboratory, where he conducted chemical experiments. He also studied physics and read philosophy.

Next day Wallace finished his calls shortly before 6 p.m. He went home for his evening meal and set out again, he was later to say, at about 6.45, to visit Mr. Qualtrough. It had stopped drizzling, so he left his mack at home and wore his overcoat and trilby hat. As he left he reminded his wife to bolt the back door after him, as she always did.

Timings now become essential in the study of this murder case. Alan Close, 14, a milk-boy, was to say later that he delivered milk to Mrs. Wallace at 6.30 that evening, and she spoke to him. Two more boys making deliveries in the street saw Close outside Wallace's home. One said this was at 6.30, the other said it was about two minutes later.

Wallace's story that he left home at 6.45 was borne out by a witness who said that at 7.10 he saw Wallace changing trams at a junction about 20 minutes' ride from his home.

It didn't take Wallace long to establish that there was no such place as Menlove Gardens East. A tram conductor told him to take a tram to Penny Lane and change. Having changed trams, Wallace asked the next conductor to put him off at Menlove Gardens West, saying that Menlove Gardens East should be nearby. "I am a complete stranger around here," he said. Neither of the tram conductors knew that there was no Menlove Gardens East.

In Menlove Gardens West, Wallace asked a passer-by, Sydney Green, to direct him. Green told him that Menlove Gardens East did not exist. Wallace then went to 25 Menlove Gardens West and asked for Mr. Qualtrough. The elderly woman who answered the door said she had never heard of him.

After walking up and down Menlove Gardens North and South, Wallace saw a policeman, explained his mission and asked him to direct him to Menlove Gardens East. The constable told him there was no such road. There were Menlove Gardens North, South and West, but not East.

When Wallace asked where he could obtain a street directory, the officer advised him to try the Allerton Road post office or the police station. Wallace glanced at his watch. He said: "Will the post office still be open? Yes, it's not eight o'clock yet, is it?"

The constable checked his own watch and replied, "That's right, it's just a quarter to."

It was later claimed that Wallace's numerous requests for directions and his checking the time with the constable were efforts to establish an alibi. He had repeatedly asked the first tram conductor not to forget to drop him at Penny Lane. Was he making sure he was remembered by as many witnesses as possible? He went to the post office, where he was told they had no directory, and he was advised to try the newsagent's across the street. Twenty-five minutes after he spoke to the policeman he was at the newsagent's trying to find Menlove Gardens East in the directory. Again he was told there was no such road. Shortly afterwards, he was later to say, he realised he had been given a false name and address. Wondering why, he became worried, because there had recently been several burglaries in Anfield, two of them in his own street. Despondent over his lack of success, he boarded the next tram and headed for home.

At 8.25 Wallace's next-door neighbour, Mrs. Florence Johnston, heard two thumps. She assumed the noise had been made by her father taking off his boots. Twenty minutes later she and her husband were about to go out. Opening their back door they saw Wallace walking down the alley behind Wolverton Street, making for his own back yard. Mrs. Johnston called out, "Good evening, Mr. Wallace."

Wallace stopped, turned and said: "I've been out this evening. Have you heard anything unusual going on in my house while I've been gone?"

"Nothing," replied Mr. Johnston. "We'll stay with you while you look around – just in case."

Wallace went round the back and the first thing he noticed was that several lights had been left on. Then, waiting outside, Mr. Johnston heard a strangled cry: "Julia!"

He ran into the house. "What is it?" he called out. "Has she fallen down the stairs?"

Wallace called out: "Come and see! She's been killed!"

Mr. Johnston found Wallace standing in the parlour, his face the colour of parchment, staring down at the body of his wife, her battered head surrounded by a halo of blood. She lay on her back on the hearthrug. The gas fire was out and her feet were near the fender, her head near the open door, her sightless eyes staring at the pedals of her piano. Her skull was split open above her left ear, revealing her brain. There was brain-matter on the floor and the wall was stippled with bloodstains, some as high as four feet.

"They've finished her!" Wallace said. "They've finished her!" He kept repeating the phrase.

As Mr. Johnston left to fetch the police, Wallace and Mrs. Johnston went into the kitchen where he pointed to a cabinet in which he kept his photographic equipment. Its door had been prised off and lay broken on the floor. Wallace then took a cash box from the shelf. It had been rifled and when Mrs. Johnston asked how much was missing, Wallace replied, "About four pounds, I think. But I can't be certain until I've checked my books." The box had contained money he had collected for his company.

He went upstairs to check the middle bedroom and found that a wad of £1 notes kept in a jar had not been touched. Rejoining Mr. Johnston in the kitchen he sat quietly for a few minutes, then returned to the parlour. Mrs. Johnston followed him. "They've finished her," he said again. "Look at the brains." Then he exclaimed in surprise, "What was she doing with my mackintosh?" Part of his raincoat could be seen beneath his wife's right shoulder.

Wallace went back into the kitchen, sat in a chair and sobbed quietly until Police Constable Frederick Williams arrived at 9.15.

"How did this happen?" asked Williams, feeling for a pulse but finding none, and noting that the corpse was still slightly warm.

"I don't know," Wallace replied. Then he described his futile trip to a non-existent address. Accompanied by Wallace, the constable searched the house. The front bedroom was in disarray. The bed was half-stripped, two of Julia's handbags and three of her hats appeared to have been tossed on to it, and its pillows lay on the floor near the fireplace. The doors of the wardrobe and the drawers of the dressing-table, however, were all shut. In the kitchen they found another of Julia's handbags – it was on a chair pushed beneath the table and was partially concealed by the tablecloth. Inside it was a pound note and some small change.

More policemen arrived, followed almost immediately by a pathologist, Professor John McFall, who examined the state of rigor mortis but did not apply the other standard test to determine time of death—the taking of the body's temperature. Of the two tests, the rigor mortis examination was the least reliable. The professor concluded that Julia Wallace died about 8 p.m. and that the first blow was struck as she sat on a chair to the left of the fireplace, her head turned as if she were speaking to someone.

Professor McFall was still examining the scene when Detective Superintendent Hubert Moore, head of Liverpool CID, arrived. Moore promptly gave orders for the city's railway station, boarding-houses, all-night cafés and clubs to be checked for a man with bloodstained clothes.

At 11.50 the body was examined by Dr. Hugh Pierce, the Liverpool police surgeon. He put the time of death at around 6 p.m. and, like McFall, he didn't take the corpse's temperature.

At the scene of crime, Professor McFall, who fancied himself as something of a private detective, thought Wallace was behaving too quietly, that his manner was too collected for someone who had just lost his wife.

"I was struck by his behaviour – it was abnormal," McFall commented. "When I was in the room examining the body and the blood, he came in smoking a cigarette and leaned over in front of the sideboard and flicked the ash into a bowl. It struck me at the time as being unusual."

Perhaps the pipe-smoking pathologist failed to appreciate that a smoker whose wife had just been murdered would feel a greater need than ever for a cigarette. Or perhaps he did not then know that Wallace was a man who had always been noted for his icy calm.

Two police officers noticed it. Detective Sergeant Bailey said: "He impressed me as being cool under any circumstances." And Detective Inspector Herbert Gold, who arrived at the house at 10.30 p.m. and found Wallace stroking Julia's cat, which had evidently found its way home, said, "He did not look like a man who had just murdered his wife."

Wallace himself was able to explain his unemotional attitude. After his trial he wrote an article in which he said: "For 40 years I had drilled myself in iron control and prided myself on never showing emotion outwardly. Stoicism is so little practised today that when seen it is called callousness."

Be that as it may, Inspector Gold was intrigued by the raincoat that Julia Wallace was lying on.

"Where did you leave it?" he asked Wallace.

"Hanging up in the hall."

Wallace agreed to go to the police station with the detectives. His hands and clothing were examined for signs of blood, but none were found. After five hours questioning the officers took him to the flat of his sister-in-law Amy in Sefton Park, because they were still conducting a search of Wallace's house. There Wallace spent the rest of the night on a sofa. At 10 o'clock next morning he reported to Liverpool police headquarters for further questioning, as requested, and was interrogated for another 12 hours.

Meanwhile, police had examined the mackintosh, which was blood-spattered and bore scorch marks. They began to suspect that Wallace had stripped himself naked, that he put on the mackintosh in order to kill his wife, and scorched it accidentally while stooping to turn off the gas fire.

Another hypothesis discussed was that Julia Wallace had slipped the mackintosh over her shoulders on going to answer a knock at the front door, and was then struck over the head and fell against the gas-fire, scorching the mack as she collapsed. This idea seemed to be supported by the fact that there were also scorch marks on her skirt.

A search for the murder weapon produced nothing, but the Wallaces' cleaner was later to testify that two items were missing from the house since her last visit on January 7th. These were a poker kept in the kitchen, and an iron bar from the sitting room which was used to clean under the gas fire. The police believed that the missing bar had been used to beat Mrs. Wallace about the head.

Evidently their search for that iron bar was not as painstaking as it might have been, for four years after the murder it was found by the subsequent tenants, concealed under the gas fire in the house. They gave it to the police, and there is now no trace of it.

When, accompanied by Inspector Gold, Wallace arrived at his sister-in-law's flat, he sank exhausted into an armchair. Amy lived with her son, Edwin, who now suggested to his uncle that he should get undressed and try to catch some sleep.

"You look as if you could do with it," Edwin added.

Wallace said in a weak voice, "I'm going to miss her so much."

Inspector Gold said briskly to Amy and her son, "There's no reason why I shouldn't take statements from you now."

When the statements were finished it was transparently obvious to the inspector that the Wallaces had led an exemplary life together. Not even a ripple disturbed the tranquillity of their marriage.

The inspector asked Wallace if his wife would have admitted anyone while he was out on business.

"No," he replied. "She wouldn't admit anyone unless she knew them personally. If anyone did call, she would show them into the parlour." He couldn't think of any trades people who were likely to have called – "and I don't know that she had any friends unknown to me."

Did he know anyone who knew he was going to the chess club that evening? Had he told anyone he was going there?

"No. I'd told no one I was going, and I can't think of anyone who knew I was going."

If the police hoped to find a motive for murder in Wallace's diaries, they were disappointed. His entries revealed only his philosophical attitude to life and a marriage of contented domesticity.

So who was Qualtrough? The police went back to that mysterious phone call. They discovered that the Liverpool Central Chess Club met in the basement premises of the City Café in North John Street. On the night of the murder, Monday, January 19th, Wallace, who was due to participate in a tournament game, left his house for the club at somewhere after a quarter to seven. His own recall was that it was at a quarter to seven; in any event, there was no dispute that he was gone from the house by seven o'clock.

While he was on his way the café's phone rang and a waitress, Gladys Harley, picked up the receiver. The caller was apparently unfamiliar with a public call box phone – he pressed button B instead of A, and had to speak to the operator, who put his call through for him. The operator noted his number, Anfield 1627, which was a phone box at the junction of Breck Road and Lower Breck Road. This was 400 yards from Wallace's home and he would have passed it on his way to play chess.

The caller asked for Mr. Wallace, and as Wallace had yet to arrive the call was taken by Samuel Beattie. He advised the caller to phone later, as Wallace was expected shortly.

"No, I'm too busy," the caller said. "I've got my girl's twenty-first birthday on, and I want to do something for her in the way of his business. I want to see him particularly."

Mr. Beattie offered to take a message, thinking that the caller wanted to take out a policy and that Wallace would be pleased to have the commission. The caller then identified himself as Mr. R. M. Qualtrough, saying he wanted Wallace to visit him the next evening at 7.30 at his house, 25 Menlove Gardens East.

Beattie noted this on the back of an envelope and gave Wallace the message when he arrived at 7.45.

The police were becoming convinced that Wallace was Qualtrough and had therefore murdered his wife. But of the two people who had spoken to him on the phone at the chess club – the waitress and the club captain – neither recognised the voice of Qualtrough as that of Wallace.

None the less their suspicions increased when they heard that Wallace had been asking Samuel Beattie if he could remember the time of Qualtrough's call to the chess club more precisely. They also learned that on meeting Beattie in the street after spending all day being questioned by detectives Wallace had said: "I have just left the police. They have cleared me."

They wondered why he said he'd been cleared when he had never been told he was a suspect. But after so many hours' interrogation, it was hardly surprising that he felt himself to be under suspicion.

Detectives next interviewed the milk-boy, Alan Close. If the boy had seen Mrs. Wallace at 6.30, as he said he had, and she had spoken to him, then her husband had up to 20 minutes to kill her, getting blood-spattered as he beat out her brains and then faking a robbery and cleaning himself up before he caught his tram. But no trace of blood was found on him, and none was found in the wastepipes or drains.

Several other youngsters were later to remark that Close had changed his story – he had last seen Mrs. Wallace at 6.45, not 6.30. With that new story in mind, seven detectives were despatched to make trial runs from Wallace's house to the tram stop, and then on to the junction where he changed trams. This established that Wallace could not have left home later than 6.49 p.m., so if the milk-boy's story were correct he had only four minutes in which to kill his wife, clean himself up, change his clothes, fake a burglary, attend to the gas lights and lock up. This would not have been possible.

The details of his statement were checked again and again. All were corroborated by witnesses. With no motive to go on, the police then seized on something in their suspect's medical history. Some years earlier one of Wallace's kidneys had been removed and a neurologist told the investigators that having only one kidney – which was now becoming troublesome – could affect Wallace mentally, prompting him to plan and commit the murder.

Then a policeman reported that he had seen Wallace in the street at about 3.30 p.m. on the day of the murder, and Wallace had seemed distressed. He was dabbing his eyes as if he had been weeping.

On February 2nd – 13 days after the crime – William Wallace was arrested and charged with his wife's murder. He replied: "What can I say in answer to this charge, of which I am absolutely innocent?"

The arrest prompted many people to believe in his guilt, so to counter that assumption his defending solicitor read an extract from Wallace's diary at his committal hearing. On March 25th, 1929, Wallace had noted: "Julia reminds me today it was fifteen years ago yesterday since we were married. Well, I don't think either of us regrets the step. We seem to have pulled well together and I think we both get as much pleasure and contentment out of life as most people."

The case against Wallace as outlined by the prosecution in his first appearance before the magistrates was riddled with errors of fact. Wallace was said to have left his home on the night of the murder "at any time from five to four minutes to seven," and the time Julia Wallace was seen by the milk-boy had mysteriously changed to 6.31 p.m.

To suit its case, the prosecution even "moved" the phone box nearer to Wallace's home, and the mystery caller – alleged to have been Wallace – was said to have used two totally different voices, one for the operator, another for Mr. Beattie. No evidence however was ever produced to substantiate this claim. There wasn't any.

Told he was being committed for trial, Wallace replied: "I plead not guilty to the charges against me. I would like to say that my wife and I lived together on the happiest terms. Our relations were of complete confidence in, and affection for, each other. The suggestion that I murdered my wife is monstrous. That I should attack and kill her is, to all who know me, unthinkable, and the more so when it must be realised that I could not possibly obtain one advantage by committing such a deed. Nor do the police suggest that I gained any advantages. On the contrary, in actual fact I have lost a devoted and loving comrade, my home life is completely broken up, and everything that I hold dear has been ruthlessly parted and torn from me. I am now to face the torture of this nerve-racking ordeal."

Wallace appeared before Mr. Justice Wright at Liverpool Assizes on April 22nd. Prosecuting, Mr. Edward Hemmerde, KC, told the jury that the murder had been meticulously planned and that Wallace's plot would never have been exposed if he had not inadvertently pressed button B instead of A when he made the phone call to set up his alibi.

It later became clear, however, that Wallace was accustomed to using pay-phones and was therefore most unlikely to have pressed the wrong button.

Mr. Hemmerde also claimed that in committing his "cleverly-planned crime" he made several mistakes. He replaced the cash-box on its shelf, something which a burglar-killer would not have troubled to do, and he removed the murder weapon, whereas a killer from outside would have left it at the scene of the crime.

Producing an iron poker which was a facsimile of the one found in Wallace's house, Mr. Hemmerde flourished it over his head and declared menacingly, "This poker, or something like it, could have done the deed."

Then, theatrically, he dropped the poker with a resounding crash, sending shock waves through the court, causing the jury almost to jump in their seats.

"Let me draw your attention to the fact that there was no blood on the stairs," he went on. "This shows that whoever did this crime was taking the most elaborate precautions.

"One of the most famous criminal trials on record is one which deals with a murderer who committed the crime while he was naked. In Wallace's case, he might well have put on the raincoat before beating his poor wife to death.

"If this man did what he is charged with doing, it is murder, foul and unpardonable. Few more brutal murders can ever have been committed."

But as the trial progressed the defence began to punch some telling holes in the Crown's case. Wallace's solicitor had found several youngsters who said that Alan Close, the milk-boy, had now told them he had seen Julia Wallace at a quarter to seven, not at 6.30, as he had originally stated. Under cross-examination the boy conceded that the time could have been between 6.30 and 6.45.

Then Samuel Beattie testified that he knew Wallace's voice well, and the voice he heard on the phone was nothing like it.

After PC James Rothewell told the court that he saw Wallace looking upset, and possibly crying, on the afternoon of the day of the murder, defence lawyer Mr. Roland Oliver, KC, called Mrs. Louisa Harrison, who Wallace had visited only minutes after the constable saw him.

"Did he appear to have been crying and dabbing his eyes with the end of his sleeve?" Mr. Oliver asked her.

"He was joking with me," Mrs. Harrison replied.

Next a locksmith testified that the locks of the front and back doors of Wallace's home were defective. Both were rusty, and the front-door lock had springs missing.

When Professor McFall gave evidence for the prosecution, he told the jury that since the night of the murder, when he first saw the body, he had revised his estimate of the time of Julia Wallace's death. He said that at 1 a.m. that night he had concluded that she had died at about 6 p.m., not 8 p.m. as he originally thought. Mr. Hemmerde asked him: "What would you regard as the possible margin of error in your calculation?" The pathologist replied that it would be no more than an hour. In other words, Julia Wallace could have been murdered as late as 7 p.m.

He added that from the number of blows the victim received, he believed the attack on her was carried out in a frenzy.

The defence seized on the point, because it was hard to imagine Wallace, criticised for being too laid-back, becoming frenzied.

Mr. Oliver asked: "If this is the work of a maniac and Wallace is a sane man, he didn't do it. Is that right?"

"He may be sane now," Professor McFall hedged.

"If he has been sane all his life, and he is sane now, it would be some momentary frenzy?"

"The mind is very peculiar."

"It is a rash suggestion, isn't it?"

"Not in the slightest. I've seen this sort of thing before, exactly the same thing."

"The fact that a man has been sane for fifty-two years and has been sane while in custody for the last three months would rather tend to prove he has always been sane, wouldn't it?"

"Not necessarily."

"Not necessarily?"

"No. We know very little about the private lives of people or their thoughts."

In his opening speech for the defence, Mr. Oliver had suggested that Wallace could not be both cool and calculating, as the prosecution claimed, and at the same time a frenzied maniac. There was no evidence that he had made the Qualtrough phone call, and he simply didn't have time to commit the murder, clean himself up and catch the tram.

A defence medical witness, Professor James Dible, told the court that because no tests of the body temperature were made by the two examining doctors, the time of death could not be established satisfactorily.

Several youngsters next gave evidence. A newspaper delivery boy said he had seen the milk-boy Alan Close on Mrs. Wallace's doorstep at 6.37 p.m. Three more juvenile witnesses said that the milk-boy had told them he had seen Mrs. Wallace at 6.45.

Mr. Oliver told the jury: "You have a crime here without a motive. You have a man here whose affection for his wife cannot be doubted. Looking at the two stories, you may think that the story of the defence does not sound very likely. But the story of the prosecution sounds impossible."

For the prosecution, Mr. Hemmerde poured scorn on the importance of the timings. "The man who made his plans, whether the boy was seen at 6.30 or 6.35 talking to this woman, had between that time and 6.49, practically twenty minutes – ample time, in my view, to commit the murder."

In his summing-up, Mr. Justice Wright appeared to come down on the side of Wallace. He said: "However you regard this matter, the whole crime was so skilfully devised and executed, and there is such an absence of any trace to incriminate anyone, as to make it very difficult to say that it can be brought home to anyone in particular. If there was an unknown murderer, he has covered up all his traces.

"Can you say that it is absolutely impossible that there was no such person? The evidence is quite consistent with some unknown criminal, for some unknown motive, having got into the house and executed the murder and gone away."

The jury, however, refused to be persuaded. After an hour's retirement they found Wallace guilty of killing his wife. Passing the death sentence, the judge made no comment, pointedly omitting to express a judge's customary agreement with the verdict.

When on May 18th, 1931, the case came to the Appeal Court, the judges were more than aware of the rumblings of public discontent over the verdict. Popular feeling had swung round in favour of Wallace and newspapers were being swamped with letters protesting about the conviction. On the eve of the appeal hearing prayers were said at a special service in Liverpool Cathedral for the appeal judges "to be guided in their judgement."

The Bishop of Liverpool commented: "There is a good deal of anxiety in this city about this case. I think it is right that people should pray like this."

At the appeal hearing Mr. Oliver told the judges: "I am entitled to insist that the prosecution prove their case. A verdict which shocks the public sense of justice cannot stand...You cannot have a man convicted of murder on this evidence."

The Lord Chief Justice agreed with him. He announced: "The conclusion we have arrived at is that the case against the appellant was not proved with the certainty which is necessary in order to justify a verdict of guilty. The appeal will be allowed and the conviction is quashed."

Wallace was released. But although his defence, financed by his union and the Prudential, had cost £1,500, the Government declined to consider compensation.

Back at his job, he found that many of his colleagues, neighbours and friends still evidently considered he was guilty and refused to speak to him. In his diary he noted: "They are the rottenest crowd I have ever struck. To go about feeling that one is shunned by nearly everyone is a terrible ordeal. The whole business depresses me beyond words."

He felt obliged to move house to Ulverston in Lancashire, and his employers found a new job for him at their Liverpool office in Dale Street.

So who was Qualtrough, if he wasn't William Wallace? A key to his identity surfaced in Walace's diary four months after the Appeal Court hearing. His entry for September 14th, 1931, noted: "As I was going to dinner X stopped me and said he wanted to talk. It was a desperately awkward situation. He must realise I suspect him of the terrible crime."

The diary did not reveal the identity of "X." But investigations after Wallace's death revealed him to be Richard Gordon Parry, a small-time crook and former colleague of Wallace, who was said to have been dismissed from the Prudential for false accounting.

Following Parry's death in 1980, a documentary programme broadcast by Merseyside's Radio City revealed that on January 22nd, 1931, three days after the murder of Julia Wallace, Wallace made a statement to the police in which he said: "Mr. Gordon Parry is a friend of my late wife and myself. He was employed by the Prudential up to about twelve or fifteen months ago. He had collected premiums which he did not pay in. He is a single man, aged 22. He took over my round when I was ill. There were discrepancies in his accounts. He visited me when I was ill in bed in the middle bedroom in 1928. I saw him in the City Café when I was playing chess there recently. We spoke."

Parry, as a family acquaintance, would have been admitted to the house by Julia Wallace without any questioning. He was familiar with Wallace's routine and habits. He would have known that when the couple went out for the evening together Wallace invariably took his collection money with him in case of burglary. Parry would also have known that on the Tuesday night – the night of the murder – there would be a considerable amount of cash in the house. So in order to get his hands on the money he would have had to separate the couple by sending Wallace off on a fool's errand. He could not have known that Wallace had collected only £4, having been ill with flu and not having made any collections the previous week. And on top of all that, Parry would have a score to settle if he believed Wallace had reported him for false accounting.

In 1965 the author Jonathan Goodman discovered that "X" was Parry and confronted him. But the suspect refused to talk and could not be identified because of the risk of libel. After Parry's death, however. Goodman named him as Julia Wallace's killer, and the Radio City investigators then made further discoveries.

They found a man named John Parkes, who was on duty at a Liverpool garage on the night of the murder. Parkes said that Parry had driven into his garage and asked him to hose down his car. Parkes said that when he was about to retrieve a bloodstained glove from inside the car, Parry snatched it from him, exclaiming, "If the police found that, it would hang me!"

Parkes said he had told Detective Superintendent Moore, who was in charge of the murder investigation, about this incident after Wallace was found guilty, but Moore had told him he must be mistaken. Further inquires by the Radio City investigators revealed that Parry's father was a senior official of Liverpool Corporation – and Superintendent Moore's daughter was employed as the secretary of that official.

Was Richard Gordon Parry therefore Qualtrough, and the killer of Julia Wallace? In 1984, Roger Wilkes, producer of the Radio City investigative programme, published an account of the case called *Wallace: The Final Verdict.* He wrote: "My researches have convinced me beyond a reasonable doubt that not only did Wallace not murder his wife, but that the prima facie case against Parry was every bit as strong as the case against Wallace, and in several important respects much more damaging."

Parry was interviewed by the police after Wallace voiced his suspicions about him. He claimed he had an alibi – he was out that evening with his girl friend. It has since been established, however, that on the night of the murder she was working until 8.30. Roger Wilkes traced her and tried to interview her, but like Parry she refused to talk.

Two years after the murder of Julia Wallace her husband's kidney complaint, which had long been troublesome, became life-threatening. Wallace, who had gradually lost the will to live, refused an operation and died on February 25th, 1933. He was buried alongside his wife.

Qualtrough – Richard Gordon Parry or whoever – had claimed his second victim, destroying William Wallace just as surely as he had killed the insurance agent's wife.

3

LIZZIE BORDEN

Whacking her way to infamy

Whoever it was who passed on to us the legend of Lizzie Borden, one of New England's most notorious daughters, couldn't count properly. We are told:

Lizzie Borden took an axe
And gave her mother forty whacks.
When she saw what she had done
She gave her father forty-one.

In fact, Lizzie's stepmother was struck 20 times, and her father only 10. Both of them are said to have died from their daughter's murderous onslaught. But Lizzie was acquitted of her parents' murder, and many of her neighbours in Fall River, Massachusetts, flatly refusing to believe that the prim Sunday School teacher could be a double-killer.

That being so, who really did kill Mr. and Mrs. Borden? Although the murders happened in 1892, it was not until the 1960s that a convincing theory was put forward to explain them.

Despite their outward respectability in their outwardly respectable neighbourhood, the Bordens were a dysfunctional family. Andrew Borden, 70 at the time he died, was a retired undertaker who had gone in for property development and then become president of a bank. His meanness was a local legend – people said that in his undertaking days he cut off corpses' feet in order to squeeze their bodies into undersized coffins.

Although he was worth half a million dollars – a colossal fortune in the 1890s – his modest detached house was lit only by kerosene lamps, and he often sat in the dark in order to save on lighting costs.

The plumbing arrangements in the house were rudimentary, with no running hot water. Newspapers were recycled as lavatory paper and Andrew Borden collected all the rents from his slum tenants himself, selling his spare eggs from a wicker basket on his rounds.

His second wife Abby, 65, was equally eccentric. She was a compulsive eater, and gluttony had made her a recluse. She was only five feet tall compared with her husband's gaunt six-foot-two, but she weighed more than 14 stone.

Lizzie adored her father – or at least she did until she reached her middle twenties. When she graduated from high school she presented him with a symbolic gift – her graduation ring. She placed it on his little finger and he wore it for the rest of his life.

In contrast, she had not spoken to her stepmother for years, and nor had her sister Emma. The cause of the rift was that their father had bought a small property, putting it in their stepmother's name without telling them.

Lizzie, 32, and Emma, ten years her senior, were furious about that because they regarded stepmother Abby as their rival for their father's affection. When they learned of the property deal they felt it had been done behind their backs, and that it showed that their father cared more for his second wife than he did for his own two daughters. From that time on they seldom ate meals with their parents.

Old Andrew Borden was somewhat taken aback by his daughters' overt hostility over the property deal. He tried to make amends by buying a tenanted cottage which he put in both their names. But the gesture was belated. The two girls considered he had put their stepmother first, and they had already made up their minds that she had become an evil influence on him.

They now froze Abby Borden out of their lives. That was

not all that difficult. Abby was rarely seen in Fall River, because she was so fat that she found it physically difficult to get out and about.

Her two stepdaughters occupied themselves, like many other spinsters of their day, by working for various local charities. Although Andrew Borden never gave a cent to charity himself, good causes benefited from his wealth because he was always uncharacteristically benevolent to his daughters.

Some bizarre things went on behind the closed doors of the respectable Borden family. For a long time Lizzie had been having "funny turns" which coincided with her menstrual periods and which are now believed to have been epileptic.

She didn't foam at the mouth in fits, but epilepsy is not always convulsive. It occurs in a variety of forms, and Lizzie Borden's spasms lasted for no more than an hour, during which she would seem withdrawn and would behave strangely.

Her "turns" probably account for a senseless theft she committed in her own home, a robbery quickly detected by her father who called the police. Lizzie showed them a nail protruding from the lock of the back door, indicating how the thief must have broken in. But they suspected an inside job and her father pursued the matter no further when he realised that Lizzie was responsible.

Her behaviour at such times was sufficiently weird for some to consider her mildly crazy, and after this incident her father kept his bedroom door locked. He left the key on the mantelpiece of another room as a reproving hint to Lizzie.

Then in the summer of 1892 Lizzie Borden went shopping for poison. But when she said she needed prussic acid for cleaning a sealskin cape, several chemists refused to sell it to her. They knew that there is no such use for prussic acid.

Shortly afterwards both Mr. and Mrs. Borden fell ill. Abby complained to a doctor that she was being poisoned, and Lizzie told a friend that she suspected that either the bread from the baker was contaminated or someone was putting poison in the can the family put out each night for the next morning's delivery of milk.

Little significance was attached to this curious event after the Bordens died their horrific death, because the murder weapon was a hatchet. It is now believed, however, that Lizzie was planning to murder her stepmother with poison. And she had a motive, although this was unappreciated at the time.

Her father was about to sell a farm which the family used as a holiday retreat. This property too was in Abby's name, and although the buyer was the girls' uncle, John Morse, who would let the family continue to use the farm for their holidays, Andrew Borden knew that his daughters would resent the sale. He tried to keep it secret, but Lizzie, who kept her ear to the ground, probably got wind of it.

Uncle John Morse visited the Bordens' home on Wednesday, August 3rd, 1892. He expected the two sisters to be away, for Emma was staying with friends and Lizzie had gone away on holiday too. Andrew Borden felt confident that the transaction could be completed during his daughters' absence, but he was in for a shock.

For that afternoon Lizzie cut short her holiday and returned home earlier than expected. She greeted her parents and Uncle John coldly, and as soon as she had unpacked her things she went out to visit an elderly neighbour and friend, Alice Russell.

She told Miss Russell: "I am afraid someone will do something...I feel as if something is hanging over me that I can't shake off." She feared that the family was being poisoned, and said she thought her father had an enemy. She spoke of seeing a man loitering near the house one night, and disclosed that the place had been robbed in broad daylight. When, somewhat surprised, Miss Russell said she had not heard of this, Lizzie explained, "Father forbade our telling of it." She was referring to the robbery she herself was suspected of committing.

The next morning dawned hot and bright. Uncle John Morse, who had stayed overnight in the Bordens' guest room, was the first to leave the house for a business meeting. Andrew Borden went out a little later, and Abby got herself ready to meet Uncle John Morse at the lawyer's office, where they had an appointment for her to sign over her holiday property. Lizzie joined the family's maid Bridget Sullivan in the kitchen for coffee. Then Abby told Bridget to clean the windows, and the maid went outside with a bucket and mop, saying that she would refill the bucket from an outside tap, so Lizzie could lock the back door.

That left Lizzie alone in the house with her stepmother. Bridget, cleaning the windows from outside, paused only for a chat over the fence with the maid next-door. She could see into the ground-floor rooms of the Borden house as she cleaned the windows, and noticed nobody inside, and during that time she saw no one leave or enter. Yet at about 9.30 that morning Abby Borden was bludgeoned to death with an axe in the upstairs guest-room, just vacated by Uncle John Morse, and a woman neighbour saw the room's shutters suddenly close. The neighbour thought this was strange on such a hot day.

At 10.45 Andrew Borden came home earlier than anticipated and found that his key wouldn't open the front door. Bridget, now back in the house, heard him fumbling at the door, and as she went to unlock it she heard Lizzie giggle upstairs. Borden came in, asked where his wife was, and Bridget heard Lizzie say, "She had a note from a sick friend and had to go out. I don't know who it was who wanted her."

Throughout the rest of the proceedings, her arrest and trial, Lizzie was to stick with that strange story of the unknown caller who brought the sick note, despite the fact that it was clear her stepmother never left the house.

After going upstairs to his bedroom Andrew Borden returned downstairs and laid on the sitting-room sofa. Bridget went upstairs to her room to lie down, still suffering from after-effects of the poisoning that had afflicted the household. Then at about 11.15 she heard Lizzie call, "Come down, quick! Father's dead. Somebody came in and killed him!"

The maid ran downstairs, saw her employer's body on a sofa in the living-room, and was immediately asked by Lizzie to run and fetch a doctor. Bridget returned moments later with Dr. Bowen from across the street, and while he examined Andrew Borden, Bridget asked, "Miss Lizzie, where was you? Didn't I leave the screen door locked?"

Lizzie replied that she had been out in the back yard, heard a groan and came in. The screen door, she said, was wide open.

Dr. Bowen emerged from the sitting-room. Mr. Borden, he said, had been murdered. Bridget volunteered to fetch Abby from the lawyer's office where, she knew, her mistress had an appointment that morning.

"I am almost positive I heard her coming in," said Lizzie. "Won't you go upstairs to see?"

Before the maid could take a step a neighbour arrived at the house, and Lizzie and the visitor went upstairs together. They found Abby's body in the guest-room. She lay on the floor, her skull crushed, exposing her brain.

Lizzie became hysterical. "I can't be left alone in this house," she cried, and pleaded with Bridget to fetch Alice Russell. She had to be sedated by Dr. Bowen, and was put to bed.

Four police officers arrived shortly afterwards. They and Dr. Bowen saw at once that Mrs. Borden had been killed much earlier than her husband. Her blood had gone dark and congealed, whereas Andrew Borden's was still flowing. Post-mortems later confirmed this – Abby Borden died about 90 minutes before her husband. John Morse arrived as the police began their investigation. Because he had stayed in the house that night, he was initially a suspect. His detailed alibi, with plenty of witnesses, suggested that he had feared something might happen.

The police asked themselves what kind of killer would have entered the locked house unobserved in broad daylight, murdered Mrs. Borden, waited an hour and a half undisturbed, killed Mr. Borden, and then slipped away unseen without taking anything. They decided it had to be an inside job – there was no other credible explanation.

The only person known to have been alone with both victims was their daughter Lizzie. The police officers sat down in the Borden lounge and waited for Lizzie to wake up. She was their prime suspect.

When at last Lizzie came downstairs again she had changed her dress. There was no sign of blood on her, and she seemed strangely calm as she answered questions while busily giving instructions about the funeral arrangements.

Asked where she had been when her father was murdered, she said she was upstairs in the family's barn behind the house, looking for lead to make sinkers for a fishing-line. She claimed she had been there for about 30 minutes, yet there had been no sign of dust on her hands or clothes when the police first saw her. Examination of the barn's upper floor revealed that no one had been there recently. The floor was thick with dust, and any footprint would have showed.

Asked if she thought John Morse or Bridget could be involved in the murders, she shook her head. Had she any idea who could have killed her mother? "She was not my mother," she replied. "She was my stepmother. My mother died when I was a child."

The police looked in vain for a tell-tale bloodstained dress, but they were more successful in their search for the murder weapon. They found an axe-head in the cellar, its handle newly broken. It seemed that someone had rubbed ash over it to make it appear unused, and it fitted the wounds made on both victims.

The police made no move to arrest Lizzie. They presented their report to the district attorney, who advised that Lizzie should remain at home until further notice for her own safety. The same advice was also given to Emma when she arrived home.

When the town's chief of police and the mayor conveyed this request, Lizzie demanded: "Why? Is anyone in this house suspected?"

"Well, Miss Borden," the mayor replied. "I regret to answer but I must answer. Yes, you are suspected."

Bridget the maid moved out of the house to a new job in the town, and Alice Russell moved in to look after the sisters. The day after the murders Lizzie and Emma offered a $5,000 reward to "anyone who may secure the arrest and conviction of the person who occasioned the deaths of Mr. Andrew Borden and his wife." They also hired a private detective.

On August 6th Alice Russell was in the kitchen when Lizzie walked in with a dress. "This old dress is covered with paint," she said. "I'm going to burn the old thing." She began tearing it up and burning it.

Alice Russell watched fearfully. "I wouldn't let anyone see me doing that if I were you," she said.

Five days later, on August 11th, Lizzie was arrested and charged with murdering her father. She pleaded not guilty at her arraignment, and was later charged with her stepmother's murder. At her subsequent trial the judges ruled that as she was effectively under arrest when she was told not to leave the house, whatever she said after that time was inadmissible because she had not been cautioned that she need not say anything.

An initially hostile press now swung round in her favour. One newspaper offered a $500 reward to the person who brought the sick-note which Lizzie claimed had been delivered at the house for Abby, but nobody came forward. At her trial the prosecution were to suggest that the note never existed.

Lizzie was always a diligent churchgoer, and church leaders described her arrest as "an outrage." As her trial approached her case attracted so much public sympathy that the attorney-general became nervous. He claimed he was ill and appointed a deputy to prosecute.

Five days before the trial began on Monday, June 5th, 1893, while Lizzie was still being held in jail, another woman in Fall River was murdered by an unknown axe-man. It seemed like a bizarre coincidence if two axe-killers were at large in the same town at the same time, and her lawyers made the most of it.

The defence team also had an influential advantage. One of them, the eloquent George D. Robinson, was a former governor of Massachusetts who had appointed one of the three trial judges as a Superior Court judge. Justice Dewey therefore owed Lawyer Robinson a favour, and when Dewey summed up at the end of the trial, he virtually recommended Lizzie's acquittal.

The defence claimed that as Andrew Borden had made no will, Lizzie had no motive, and the maid, Bridget Sullivan, testified that she could not recall which dress Lizzie wore on the morning of the murders. It was afterwards claimed, however, that the maid was paid for her testimony—she subsequently returned to her native Ireland with enough money to buy a farm.

Alice Russell, the only witness who could remember the burnt dress, said it had been light blue with a dark blue pattern—just like the dress Lizzie had destroyed three days after the murders, saying, "I'm going to burn the old thing," although she had had it for only five months. Emma Borden, however, testified that she had asked Lizzie to burn the dress, which had paint on it. Emma said she had asked Lizzie to get rid of it because she herself wanted more room to hang her own clothes.

Asked if her relationship with her stepmother had been cordial, Emma replied, "Well, we never felt that she was much interested in us, and at one time Father gave her some property and we felt that we ought to have some too."

The court was told that doctors decapitated both victims during the post-mortems in order to remove the flesh from the skulls so that they could examine the wounds.

With what can only be described as remarkable insensitivity, the medical experts then produced the two skulls in court, whereupon Lizzie fainted.

The judges ruled that evidence that she had tried to buy prussic acid was inadmissible because it had nothing to do with a double murder where the weapon used was clearly an axe.

Throughout her trial Lizzie spoke only 13 words: "I am innocent. I leave it to my counsel to speak for me."

After retiring for just one hour on the thirteenth day, the jury returned with a verdict of not guilty. The court erupted into tumultuous applause, but the verdict left an awkward question unanswered.

If Lizzie didn't kill her parents, who did? No other killer seemed conceivable, and Lizzie had both the time and a motive. Nobody else was near enough to hear the thud as her stepmother's body hit the floor, and the first blow could have prevented any scream Abby might have given. Lizzie then had about 20 minutes in which to kill her father as he snoozed on the sofa. One of the 10 blows he received was delivered with enough force to cut an eyeball in two and slice through a cheekbone.

With such a blow the hatchet's handle could well have snapped, and all she then had to do was put the handle in the stove, smear the axe-head with ash, pop it in a box with other dusty hatchets, change her dress and clean herself up.

Her father had taken off his coat on entering the house. He usually hung it up, but it was found crumpled under his head on the sofa. So did Lizzie wear it to stop his blood spattering her clothes?

Although acquitted, she remained notorious for the rest of her life. Inheriting their father's fortune, the sisters sold their home and bought a larger house in the town's most exclusive district. Eleven years later Lizzie met an actress she admired, Nance O'Neill, and brought her home as a house guest. Wild parties ensued, resulting in Emma's departure, and a lesbian relationship between Lizzie and the actress was rumoured.

Before she left for good Emma was asked in an interview if she had ever thought her sister guilty. "No, and again no," she replied.

The axe-head found by the police was never positively proved to be the murder weapon, and Emma added: "Here is the strongest thing which had convinced me of Lizzie's innocence. The authorities never found the axe, or the implement or whatever it was which figured in the killings. If Lizzie had done that deed she could not have hidden the instrument of death so that the police would never find it. Time and again she has avowed her innocence to me, and I believe her."

Lizzie Borden died at her home in 1927 following an operation from which she never fully recovered. And when Emma read of her sister's death, she fell, broke her hip and died 10 days later. The sisters were buried in the family plot at a local cemetery, joining the remains of their father, mother and stepmother.

There has since been no shortage of theories attempting to solve the double murder. Ed McBain, author of the 87th Precinct novels, has suggested that the maid Bridget Sullivan and Lizzie were having a lesbian affair and killed Andrew Borden when he threatened to expose them.

A more plausible analysis of the case came in 1967 from Victoria Lincoln in her book *A Private Disgrace: Lizzie Borden by Daylight*. The author had grown up in Fall River, knew Lizzie and had relatives who were associates of Lizzie's father.

Lizzie was menstruating at the time of the murders, and Victoria Lincoln's book suggests that Abby was killed during one of Lizzie's epileptic spasms, which coincided with her periods. This would explain the strange timing of the murder—in broad daylight, with Bridget around and discovery possible at any moment.

Victoria Lincoln believes that Lizzie didn't know what she was doing, like many another epileptic experiencing such a spasm, and she had no recollection of it. But she realised what had happened, and knew that she must be responsible. Her father had protected her over the burglary, but she knew he couldn't and wouldn't extricate her from his wife's murder. Lizzie couldn't face seeing his affection turn to condemnation, so she axed him to death while he still loved her. As he was asleep, he never knew who or what hit him. Then Lizzie did her best to cover her tracks.

There are numerous examples of epileptics fulfilling deep-seated ambitions they would never have had the courage to achieve during normal consciousness. Victoria Lincoln cites a skier who felt an attack coming on as he set off down a difficult slope. When he returned to normality his tracks showed him that he had made the descent flamboyantly, taking a route over rough terrain he would never normally have had the nerve to negotiate.

The author also gives an instance of the case of a young man who "woke" in his office knowing he had just had an attack. He discovered how remarkable this had been a few days later when his salary was raised. His boss, faced with the young man's lucidly expressed case for a rise, and his threat to quit unless he got one, had been favourably impressed.

Lizzie Borden apparently toyed with the idea of poisoning her stepmother, making the whole family ill in the process and trying unsuccessfully to buy prussic acid. Poison is a woman's weapon. An axe isn't. So did Lizzie's desire to see Abby dead take over uncontrollably during an epileptic spasm?

One thing is certain. No woman would calmly axe her parents to death in mid-morning daylight when she was not even alone with them – unless she had temporarily taken leave of her senses.

4

GEORGE JEFFREYS

A not so bloody judge

James Duke of Monmouth fancied himself as the king of England. He was the bastard son of Charles II – his mother was the king's mistress Lucy Walters – and when his father died the natural heir to the throne was the King's brother James.

It was at that point that Monmouth said to himself, "If Uncle James can be king, why not me?" He was forgetting perhaps, that Englishmen did not like sons to succeed who were born on the wrong side of the blanket – there were far too many of them.

Monmouth, 36 years old, had little to recommend him apart from his charm and a striking appearance. But he had friends who came to see him in Holland, to where he had fled after the failure of one of his plots, urging him to have a tilt at the crown. They didn't so much as want Monmouth for king as not want his uncle, who they detested.

So it was that in 1685, shortly after his uncle had been proclaimed King James II, Monmouth landed at Lyme Regis and was hailed as King Monmouth in the western counties. With a rabble of half armed and untrained men he led an attack on the royal troops at Sedgemoor during the night of July 5th - 6th and was hopelessly defeated. The man who would be king fled to the New Forest, but was captured at Ringwood. He was taken before his uncle where he fell grovelling on his knees, pleading for his life.

The new King, though, had no mercy for traitors, especially those who were related to him. King Monmouth was taken to Tower Hill and beheaded on July 15th.

Then the King sent a note to his Lord Chief Justice, Baron George Jeffreys.

"Go West and deal with the captured rebels," the King said. "There is to be no mercy shown."

Some historians would have us believe that the King knew exactly what he was doing when he picked George Jeffreys to hold his "Bloody Assizes" across England's western counties. As a result Jeffreys has endured a 300-year reputation for courtroom cruelty and callousness that has no equal. Hectoring witnesses, scoffing at captured rebels, Jeffreys, we are told, ordered hundreds of instant hangings, the bodies afterwards being cut up and exhibited on posts to remind the fearful populace of the fate of those who dared rebel against their lawful King.

But was Judge Jeffreys really as bad as all that?

In peeling away the myths that surround him, several things need to be borne in mind. First, there was nothing unusual about his sentencing policy – it was the order of the day. Second, popular historians have treated him a bit like an Aunt Sally, because his portrayal as a thorough villain went down well with readers, particularly those who didn't like James II. Third, Jeffreys became notorious only because he had to do an unpleasant job.

None of this makes him whiter than white, but it helps to put his bad press in perspective. The death sentences passed by Jeffreys after the rebellion were not individually extraordinary – execution was the standard penalty for high treason. It was the sheer number of those executions that caused the episode to become known as the Bloody Assizes. And to this day no one is quite sure about the total. Some accounts put the figure at 300, others estimate up to 800.

What is probably the most accurate figure was not computed until 1929, when the historian J. G. Muddiman examined the original judges' lists sent to the Treasury on November 12th, 1685. From these documents it appears that 321 executions took place during the Bloody Assizes, and about 165 further executions connected with the rebellion were carried out later.

If Judge Jeffreys were today called to account for all this, he could argue that he was only obeying the King's orders. Following Monmouth's defeat, Colonel Kirke, the Royalist military commander in charge of the West Country, had already begun the summary execution of rebel prisoners, which was standard practice in such situations.

Then King James ordered the military executions to be stopped. He wanted to make a more public example of those rash enough to rise up against their lawful king, so he decreed that all the rebels should be tried at the next assizes.

That was all very well in theory, but it was impossible to give hundreds of rebels a fair trial in the five weeks allotted to the assizes. If many of the prisoners pleaded not guilty the process could take years. But as far as the King was concerned, that was the judges' problem. They must get on with it and be quick about it.

He appointed five of them, headed by George Jeffreys, who despite being only in his mid-thirties was a sick man racked with pain from gallstones. He was in Tunbridge Wells, receiving treatment for his complaint, when he got the King's call. He set out for the West Country to do his best – or his worst, depending how you look at it.

If he had refused to co-operate, he could himself have been indicted for high treason. He could of course have ducked out of those assizes on health grounds. Why didn't he? The answer no doubt was that he was an ambitious man, seeking further preferment – he had his eye on the post of Lord Chancellor.

For three centuries historians portrayed Jeffreys as the bully of the bench, pressurising juries to bring in quick convictions. Long after he was dead and therefore unable to correct the calumnies, those historians put words into his mouth that he never spoke. Upon instructing a hangman to whip a woman offender, he was quoted as saying: "Scourge her soundly, man! Scourge her till the blood runs down! It is Christmas, a cold time for Madam to strip in. See that you warm her shoulders thoroughly!"

Turn to the trial transcript, however, and you discover that what Jeffreys actually said was: "Scourge her soundly, and since she has a mind to it in this cold weather, let her be well heated." Then, turning to the woman, Jeffreys simply recited the standard pronouncement: "Your sentence is that you be taken to the place from whence you came, and from thence dragged tied to a cart's tail through the streets, your body being stripped from the girdle upwards, and be whipt till your body bleeds."

These were the words that every judge used in such a case, yet for uttering them Jeffreys was said to have pronounced the sentence with "a fiendish exultation." And as the speech wasn't quite colourful enough for the historians, they rewrote it to make it more brutal. Accorded such treatment by the chroniclers, it is small wonder that Judge Jeffreys was labelled in such an unsavoury manner by posterity.

The Bloody Assizes began at Winchester, the first stop on the judges' circuit, with the high-profile trial of Dame Alice Lisle, aged about 70 and the widow of John Lisle, a judge who had been elevated to the peerage by Oliver Cromwell after helping to try King Charles I. Later on in Cromwell's time, Lisle had presided over a Commonwealth court which condemned several royalists to death for treason, including a clergyman who refused to plead and was sent to the scaffold without a hearing. After the restoration of the monarchy Lisle subsequently fled abroad and was assassinated by royalists.

This background made his widow Alice a natural suspect, for she was clearly seen as no friend of the monarchy. It is believed that King James expected her to be convicted, and that Jeffreys sensed that he would be in trouble if she wasn't.

This may well have been so, but it stops far short of what

some accounts claim happened at the trial. One early historian, writing about 20 years after the event, recorded that "though the jury brought her [Dame Alice] in three times not guilty, yet Jeffreys' threats so far prevailed that she was at last found guilty of high treason and beheaded for it."

This is simply not true, as transcripts of the trial show. They demonstrate that although Jeffreys' conduct of the trial was not impeccable, he did not hector the jury. He merely directed their attention to the incriminating evidence given by a witness. This testimony clearly indicated that Dame Alice was guilty, and Jeffreys felt it necessary to remind the jury of this, sending them out to deliberate further.

Moreover, but for Judge Jeffreys' advice to the prisoner, she would have suffered an even worse fate than she did. Instead of being beheaded, she would have been burned at the stake. Jeffreys saved her from that out of compassion – hardly the act of a man steeped in cruelty.

Let us see what happened ...

For 20 years Alice Lisle had lived quietly at her home, Moyles Court, near Ringwood, in the New Forest. She was highly regarded by her neighbours, despite her sympathy for dissenters – those refusing to conform to the established church.

After Monmouth's defeat at the Battle of Sedgemoor, two of his supporters, John Hicks, a dissenting clergyman, and Richard Nelthorpe, a barrister, fled from the battlefield and hid at the home of James Dunne, a baker at Warminster, 25 miles from Ringwood.

Evidently neither of the two fugitives were happy with their refuge in Dunne's bakery, so from their hiding place John Hicks wrote a letter to his friend Dame Alice asking her if she would shelter him and his companion Nelthorpe.

The baker Dunne agreed to take the letter to Ringwood. He set out to walk the 25 miles but soon lost his way. At Stoke Mandeville he asked directions from a labourer,

John Barter, who cheerfully agreed to accompany him to Moyles Court.

There Dunne delivered the letter to Dame Alice, slyly watched by Barter. Dame Alice told Dunne she would be happy to give the two men shelter, and Dunne returned to Warminster. Later he set off again for Moyles Court, accompanied by the two fugitives Hicks and Nelthorpe.

The day after Dunne and the two rebels arrived there, Colonel Penruddocke, a Ringwood magistrate, pounded on Mrs. Lisle's door. Half an hour passed before Dame Alice opened it, and in answer to the colonel's angry demands she protested that there were no fugitives at her home.

Penruddocke didn't believe her. The house and out-buildings were searched, and Hicks and the baker Dunne were discovered hiding in the malt-house, while Nelthorpe was found in a hiding-place near one of the chimneys. The colonel took all three men and Dame Alice into custody.

What had happened was that John Barter, who had so cheerfully offered his help to Dunne on the road to Ringwood, had turned informer. After guiding Dunne to Moyles Court he went to the magistrate, telling him that he suspected that Alice Lisle was concealing two rebels. And so the old lady was brought to Winchester, to face Judge Jeffreys at the Bloody Assize, on a capital charge of committing treason by harbouring rebels.

When her trial began on August 25th, 1685, Dame Alice turned out to be not only very old but also very deaf. Jeffreys allowed her to remain seated, and a man was ordered to stand beside her to repeat the evidence in a loud voice. The court then heard witnesses who proved that Hicks had been one of Monmouth's followers. Several of them who were in the royalist army told how after being captured by Monmouth's army, they were approached by Hicks who tried to persuade them to join the rebellion.

The discovery of Hicks and Nelthope in Dame Alice's house at Moyles Court was not in dispute. But had she concealed them knowing them to be rebels? That was for the jury to decide.

James Dunne, the Warminster baker, was then called to give evidence. The prosecutor described him as an unwilling witness, so Judge Jeffreys cautioned Dunne: "I would not by any means in the world fright you into anything or any ways tempt you to tell an untruth, but provoke you to tell the truth – that is the business we come about here."

Dunne had a problem. He had been arrested at Moyles Court with the two rebels, and the spectre of the hangman's noose hung over him. He wanted to clear himself without implicating others. He said he knew nothing about Hicks and Nelthorpe, who he had never seen before they arrived at his home, and he had only done what they had asked him to do. He certainly did not know, he said, that they had been involved in the business of rebellion against the King.

This seemed implausible. Would the baker, presumably a busy man, set aside two whole days in a week to walk a total of 100 miles simply to oblige two lodgers he had never set eyes on before? Jeffreys asked him what he had got out of it.

"Nothing but a month's imprisonment, my lord," Dunne replied.

"Thou seemest to be a man of a great deal of kindness and good nature," the judge observed sarcastically. After repeating Dunne's story, Jeffreys concluded: "And all to carry a message from a man thou never knewest in thy life, to a woman thou never sawest in thy life neither ..."

Pressed for further details, Dunne became confused. "I cannot tell," he kept repeating in answer to questions. The judge ordered him to stand aside for a moment and called the informer John Barter to give evidence. Barter testified he had led Dunne to Dame Alice's house and watched Dunne hand over a letter to her in her kitchen. The baker and the lady began to laugh, and afterwards Barter asked the baker what they had been laughing about. Dunne replied that Dame Alice had asked him if Barter knew anything about the "business."

Then Jeffreys called Dunne back.

"Let my honest man, Mr. Dunne, stand forward a little," the judge said. Addressing the baker he asked, "Did you not tell Barter that you told Dame Alice when she asked whether he was acquainted with this 'business,' that he knew nothing of it?"

Without thinking, Dunne replied, "Yes, my lord. I did tell him so."

"Did you so? Then you and I must have a little further discourse. Come now and tell us, what 'business' was that?"

Dunne realised too late that he was falling into a trap. He had earlier testified that he knew of no 'business.' Desperately playing for time, he asked, "Does your lordship ask what that business was?"

"Yes. It is a plain question. What was that business that Dame Alice asked thee whether the other man knew, and then you answered her that he did know nothing of it?"

Floundering about for a convincing answer as the judge persisted, Dunne finally said that the "business" was that Hicks was a dissenter.

It was now evening time and the court had become gloomy. "Hold a candle to his face that we may see his brazen face," Jeffreys ordered. "That is all nonsense. Dost thou imagine any man hereabouts is so weak as to believe thee?"

Dunne stuck doggedly to his story. Short of admitting he was lying, there was little else he could do.

After Colonel Penruddocke had described his discovery of the two rebels, Dame Alice spoke up. "My lord," she said, "I hope I shall not be condemned without being heard."

"No, God forbid, Mistress Lisle," Jeffreys reassured her. "That was a sort of practice in your husband's time – you know very well what I mean – but God be thanked it is not so now. The King's courts never condemn without a hearing."

This was an unfortunate allusion to Judge John Lisle's

treatment of the clergyman who was condemned without a hearing after he declined to testify. As soon as Jeffreys had made the remark, he clearly regretted it. When he came to sum up at the end of the trial, he made a point of reminding the jury that nothing Judge Lisle had done had any relevance to his widow's case.

Dame Alice told the court that she had been unaware that Hicks was a Monmouth supporter. She said she thought he was just a Presbyterian who found himself in danger for his preaching.

For Jeffreys the word "Presbyterian" was like a red rag to a bull. In an extraordinary outburst his self-control and careful choice of words seemed suddenly to desert him.

"There is not one of those snivelling, lying, canting Presbyterian rascals but, one way or other, had a hand in the late horrid conspiracy and rebellion!" he raged. "Presbytery has all manner of villainy in it! Nothing but Presbytery could lead that fellow Dunne to tell so many lies as he has told here, for show me a Presbyterian and I will show you a lying knave!"

The Lord Chief Justice was celebrated for such invective. His fuse was probably shortened in this case by the pain he was suffering from the ailment which was to spread and rack him until it killed him four years later.

Summing up, Jeffreys said he thought it impossible that Dame Alice did not realise that Hicks and Nelthorpe were fugitive rebels. And if the jury did decide that she was aware of this, the judge told them, "neither her age nor her sex are to move you who have nothing else to consider but the fact you are to try."

The jury then sought guidance on a point of law. As Hicks had yet to be convicted – he was in Wells awaiting trial – was it treason to give him shelter before his conviction?

Jeffreys replied that the question of Hicks's conviction was immaterial. "If Hicks had been wounded in the rebels' army, and had come to her house and there been entertained, but had died of his wounds and so could never have been convicted, she had been nevertheless a traitor."

After deliberating for 30 minutes the jury returned to announce that they were not satisfied that Dame Alice knew Hicks was a rebel. The judge then reminded them of Dunne's evidence. "Did she not inquire of Dunne whether Hicks had been in the rebel army? And when he told her he did not know, she did not say she would refuse him if he had been there, but ordered him to come by night, by which it is evident she suspected it."

After a further 15 minutes' retirement the jury returned at midnight to find Alice Lisle guilty, and the following morning she was sentenced by Jeffreys to be burned alive – the statutory method of execution for a woman traitor. The judge told her that in normal circumstances this would take place that afternoon, "but we, the judges, shall stay in town an hour or two. You shall have pen, ink and paper brought to you and in the meantime if you employ that pen, ink and paper this hour or two well – you understand what I mean – it may be you may hear further from us deferring your execution."

Dame Alice did understand what Jeffreys meant. He was advising her to petition the King for mercy. She did so, and her execution was postponed until September 2nd, with the sentence commuted to one of beheading. When this sentence was duly carried out it was reported that "she was old and dozy and died without much concern."

The judges moved on to Salisbury, and from there to Dorchester on September 5th, where about 300 alleged rebels were to be tried in what later became the Oak Room of the Antelope Hotel. Although the first 30 defendants to appear before the court were caught re-handed with their weapons, they all pleaded not guilty. If this was to be par for the course, the assize would last for years rather than the weeks scheduled. A court official was therefore sent into the prisons to tell the defendants that their only chance of saving their lives was to plead guilty.

After that, all who pleaded not guilty but were convicted were promptly executed – "without a minute to say their prayers," according to one account. The lives of most of those who pleaded guilty were spared. That is a fact. The fiction created by more than one historian was that countless prisoners were cheated – "deluded," in the words of one writer, "into pleading guilty to their indictments for a promise of pardon," and then hanged.

By the time the Dorchester hearings ended, 250 prisoners had been condemned to death, but of these only 74 went to the scaffold. The assize court moved on to Exeter, where 40 prisoners were tried and 21 were sentenced to death, 12 of them being executed and their quartered bodies exhibited locally.

For those who suffered execution the method was barbaric. They were first hanged until they were choking, then cut down while still alive, and disembowelled, with their bowels being burned in front of them. Their heads were cut off and the bodies cut into four pieces which were stuck on poles and exhibited locally – hence, "hanging, drawing and quartering." Such displays were not unusual. What was unusual was that because so many rebels were executed, there was a considerable number of bloody remains decorating the West Country for months to come.

According to one account, the quarters of 239 executed rebels were "set up in the principal places and roads of those counties, to the terror of passengers and the great annoyance of those parts." At Taunton 139 of the 526 prisoners tried were sentenced to death. At Wells only one of the 542 defendants pleaded not guilty. He was convicted and executed the same day, and of the rest 93 were condemned to death but some were subsequently reprieved. Among those who were executed was Dame Alice Lisle's friend John Hicks, despite the efforts of his brother, the Dean of Worcester, to bribe officials to save him.

Although George Jeffreys was reviled throughout the West Country as the man who had done an unpopular King's dirty work for him, elsewhere he was regarded as a hero for so firmly stamping out the aftermath of the rebellion, thereby helping to preserve England from another civil war.

Various scurrilous pamphlets were published by Monmouth sympathisers attacking him, one of them by Hicks's son-in-law, John Tutchin, who wrote *The Protestant Martyrs, or The Bloody Assizes,* "giving an account of the lives, trials and dying speeches of all those eminent Protestants that suffered in the West of England by the sentence of that bloody and cruel Judge Jeffries." [sic].

Partisan accounts like these later fuelled the work of historians who vilified "Bloody Judge Jeffreys" – one account even claimed that he was afflicted by syphilis, making no mention of his actual affliction of gallstones. A recent account brands him "the most sadistic and fearsome judge in British history," overlooking the fact that he lived at a time less civilised than our own, when courts were often necessarily as brutal as the villains they had to deal with.

There was no doubting Jeffreys' exceptional ability. He was only 35 when he became Lord Chief Justice and his handling of the trial of Alice Lisle demonstrated his skill as an inquisitor and as a judge who would not allow any witness to pull wool over his eyes. The King must have thought so too, for on his return to London Jeffreys called on James II with his report, and was rewarded with the Lord Chancellorship. By any standards this was a meteoric career, but it was to sputter out like a spent firework when his royal patron was forced to flee the country in 1688 before the arrival of William of Orange.

With this change in the monarchy Jeffreys, seen as the principal tool of a now discredited and loathed administration, became a wanted man. Disguising himself as a seaman he tried to flee the country, but was recognised and arrested at a pub called the Old Town of Ramsgate, in Wapping. He was imprisoned in the Tower of London where, in 1689, he died at the age of 40 from a kidney ailment.

True to form, his detractors pursued him beyond the grave, inventing a variety of stories about what happened to his corpse. It was said that his body was taken to

Dorchester, where it was walled up in the building where Monmouth's supporters were sentenced.

Another account claimed that he was beheaded at Taunton market place, his corpse then being interred at Stocklinch. In fact Jeffreys was first buried in the Tower Chapel, near the remains of the Duke of Monmouth, and three years later reinterred at the Church of St. Mary, Aldermanbury, in the City of London.

In his will he wrote that despite his long illness he had hoped to recover sufficiently to prove that, "I never deserved to lie under the heavy censures I now do." And up to a point, he was right. He was not quite the nasty piece of work that became his popular image.

5

EDGAR ALLAN POE

The vanishing shop-girl

For shop-girl Mary Rogers, celebrity was the stuff of dreams. She had no reason at all to imagine that she would one day have her own small corner of fame. The only trump card life had dealt her was that she was a stunningly beautiful blue-eyed brunette – and in the middle of the nineteenth century, unlike today, beautiful women didn't achieve fame for their beauty alone.

The customers who arrived to buy their cigars in the Broadway, Manhattan, tobacconist's shop where she worked loved Mary. They eschewed other cigar shops just so that they could ogle her behind her counter.

That brought a ready smile to the face of the shop-owner, John Anderson, who recognised that his eye-catching assistant was good for sales. He knew that his cigars were neither better nor cheaper than anyone else's, and that Mary was the shop's main attraction.

One of the regular customers had himself attained celebrity. He was the thriller writer Edgar Allan Poe. It is thanks to him that Mary Rogers is remembered to this day.

Although Mary had a smile for everyone, her customers got nowhere if they tried to date her. And recognising his asset, John Anderson ensured that none of them got heavy-handed after closing time.

When the shop shut for the night he made sure she was safely escorted to her home where she lived with her widowed, semi-invalid mother.

Then something extraordinary happened. One day early in 1841 Mary Rogers simply vanished.

Her mother, visited by a worried Anderson, was bewildered. She had no idea where her dutiful daughter could have gone. All she knew was what Anderson told her: he had sent Mary on a 10-minute errand along Broadway and she hadn't come back.

A week of anxiety and sadness passed. Then something equally extraordinary happened. Mary came back, with scarcely a word about where she had been.

"I decided to go and stay with friends in the country for a week," she said simply. "I felt I needed a break." No more than that.

John Anderson didn't ask questions. He was so relieved to have her back he was prepared to forgive and forget her unannounced absence. Mary didn't say where her hosts lived or who they were, and with no more ado she began to arrange a new batch of cigars on the shelves just as if nothing had happened.

Life in the tobacconist's shop soon returned to its humdrum routine. The biggest excitement in Mary's life now was the return of her brother from South America. He had prospered sufficiently to hand his mother enough cash to buy her own house, an occasion for much excitement in the Rogers' family.

Mrs. Rogers chose a property in Nassau Street, Manhattan, and decided to turn it into a boarding-house, taking in lodgers. When her son departed again on his travels, the work in the boarding-house soon proved too much for her. Regretfully, Mary gave in her notice at the tobacconist's,. explaining that she would now have to help her mother run the place, which was providing them with more than enough income to live on.

Among the first boarders at Nassau Street were two handsome young bachelors, David Payne and Alfred Crommelin. Both of them fell in love with Mary.

The two men couldn't have been more different. David

Payne did occasional work as a cork-cutter, but spent most of his time drinking in saloons around the Bowery. He could never be relied upon to keep appointments or to turn up punctually for meals.

In contrast, Alfred Crommelin had established his own business. He never drank, and he was ambitious.

Mary didn't take long to show which of the two young men she favoured. It was not diligent, dependable, happy-go-lucky Alfred Crommelin, but unpredictable, hard-drinking David Payne.

When she accepted Payne's proposal Crommelin decided to leave the boarding-house. He told Mary that as he couldn't have her, he couldn't bear to remain under the same roof. But if she were ever in trouble she had only to come to him and he'd do his best to help.

On Sunday, July 25th, 1841, Mary rose early and put on several petticoats despite the summer heat. Even more than usually well-turned-out, she put on her blue bonnet, tied its ribbons under her chin and slipped on her fawn gloves.

Then, Payne was later to say, at 10 a.m. she knocked on the door of his room. He was shaving, and when he answered the door his face was covered with lather.

Mary said: "I'm off to spend the day with my cousin Mrs. Downing. She lives on Jane Street. I'll be back this evening by the seven o'clock stage." She gave him a kiss on his lathered cheek. "Will you meet me at Broadway and Ann Street?"

Payne said he would, and he meant it, he was later to claim. But the sun got up and the day turned into a scorcher. One thirst-quenching drink led to another, and by the late afternoon he was intoxicated. He was sober enough, however, to realise that it wouldn't do for Mary to see him drunk, so he decided not to meet her.

At 5 p.m. there was a distinct change in the weather. The sky darkened and there were distant rumbles of thunder. As heavy rain threatened, Payne thought Mary would probably decide to spend the night at her cousin's. After another drink or three he went back to the boarding-house, arriving there at nine o'clock.

There was no sign of Mary, but her mother wasn't worried. Like Payne, she assumed that her daughter had decided to stay with her cousin rather than risk getting soaked in a sudden downpour.

Mary hadn't returned when Payne left for work the next morning. This wasn't all that surprising at that early hour, but when he came home for lunch and there was still no sign of her he became worried. Deciding to take the afternoon off – not a difficult decision for David Payne – he went to Jane Street to call on Mrs. Downing and to ask what had happened to Mary. To his surprise, she said that Mary had neither called nor been expected.

Payne went back to the boarding-house and consulted Mrs. Rogers. Both were aware that in the mid-1800s the overnight disappearance of a mature woman did not rate as a police matter. Mary was 21 and well able to take care of herself, and she had clearly not told the truth about her intentions for that day. Even so, they were concerned and on Payne's suggestion they decided to place a missing person advertisement for Mary in the *New York Sun*.

When the advertisement was published in the Tuesday edition of the newspaper, it was spotted by Alfred Crommelin, and he too became anxious. He became more than anxious in fact – he was conscience-stricken.

For the day previous to Mary's disappearance he had returned to his office to find that she had called in his absence, writing her name on the slate left by his door for messages. Furthermore, a fresh red rose had been pushed into his door's key-hole.

Did this mean Mary was inviting him to renew his courtship? Studying the message and the rose on that day, he could not be sure. Rather than suffer further disappointment, he decided to await a more positive approach. But now that Mary had vanished he reproached himself. She must have come to him for help, he thought, and he had let her down.

Alfred Crommelin didn't go to bed that night. Instead he scoured the city for Mary. At lunch-time the next day he was checking the Hudson River dockland where he questioned some boatmen. They told him that a woman's body had been found in the river off Hoboken, New Jersey, early that morning. The fishermen who discovered it had towed it to Hoboken, where the coroner had examined it and decided that she had been murdered. The woman hadn't been identified, and she was thought to have been killed around Sunday.

Crommelin promptly caught the ferry to Hoboken. At the morgue the coroner permitted him to view the body. Although the woman's features had been distorted by immersion and a savage beating, Crommelin instantly recognised her as Mary Rogers. She still wore her blue bonnet, and the coroner said her hands had been bound with rope. She had been raped, probably by more than one man, but prior to that she had been a virgin. She had been strangled with a strip torn from one of her petticoats.

Crommelin returned to New York with Mary's bonnet and a piece of lace from her petticoat. Her despairing mother found it difficult to believe that her daughter was dead, but there was no arguing with the bonnet and lace that Crommelin handed her. Mrs. Rogers had made the bonnet herself, as well as the lace from the petticoat. She couldn't imagine who Mary might have gone to see on the pretext of visiting her cousin.

The police discovered that a girl matching Mary's description was seen at the corner of Ann Street and Theatre Alley shortly after Mary left the boarding-house on Sunday. The girl seemed to be waiting for someone, and was eventually joined by a tall, dark young naval officer. The couple then walked off towards the Hudson River.

A man named Adams, who drove a stage between the Hoboken terminus of the New York ferry and a popular picnic riverside area known as the Elysian Fields, came forward as a witness. He recalled picking up a girl resembling Mary Rogers at the ferry at about midday on Sunday. She was accompanied by a tall, dark young man, but whether or not this companion had been in naval uniform (like the man seen meeting the girl in New York) Adams couldn't remember. Asked by detectives to think hard about that, he decided that the man was probably not in uniform.

At the Elysian Fields the investigators interviewed a Mrs. Loss, who had a refreshment stall there at a spot called Sybil's Cave. She said that a girl and young man who arrived on Adams's stage at around 1 p.m. stopped at her stall for a cool drink. They then strolled off hand-in-hand to the nearby woods. Shortly afterwards Mrs. Loss heard a woman's scream. It came from the direction of the woods, but she thought nothing of it, she said, because "girls around here are always screaming." Like Adams, she couldn't remember if the man was in uniform.

The investigation wasn't getting anywhere when New York police received an anonymous letter, which they deduced was written by two men. The writers said they knew "the beautiful Broadway cigar girl' and they had seen her at the Elysian Fields during the afternoon on Sunday.

While they were there they watched a boat arrive from the New York side of the river. It contained Mary Rogers and six young men, all well dressed. When the boat beached, the party ran happily into the woods.

A second boat then arrived, with three well-dressed young men on board who inquired after the party that had preceded them. Told where they had gone, the three men asked if the girl had gone willingly. She had appeared to do so, they were assured, and the three men then also went into the woods.

Who were the six men, and the three men who followed soon after them? There were no clues, no one could remember anything more specific about that busy summer afternoon. The police turned to the people they did know.

Mrs. Loss, the woman who owned the refreshment stall, was accused of inventing her story to boost her business, and both Crommelin and Payne became suspects: Crommelin because Mary had rejected him, and Payne because the story of the red rose left at Crommelin's office suggested that she might have been about to give Payne's rival fresh encouragement.

Both men, however, had solid alibis. Crommelin was at church on Sunday morning and spent the afternoon with a group of deacons; Payne was able to direct the police to one bartender after another, all of whom recalled him being in their saloons at various times all through that Sunday. This accounted for his movements that day until he arrived back at the boarding-house, where he had Mary's mother as a witness.

An informer then advised the investigators to check on a man named Joseph Morse, a wood-engraver who lived on Nassau Street not far from Mrs. Rogers's boarding-house.

Apparently, since the discovery of Mary's body, Mr. Morse had disappeared both from his home and his workplace. On the Sunday evening of the murder he had come home in something of a hurry, quarrelled with his wife, given her a beating, and after packing a few essentials, left. He had not been seen since.

The police began questioning Morse's friends. Some of them remembered seeing him walking along the New York waterfront on the day of Mary's disappearance, accompanied by a girl who looked remarkably like the murder victim. The couple made inquiries about ferries and then continued their stroll.

Detectives eventually traced Joseph Morse to a hotel in West Boylston, Massachusetts. He had shaved off his whiskers and was living there under an assumed name. A search of his pockets revealed newspaper cuttings about Mary's murder, mailed to him by one of his workers.

Taken back to New York police headquarters for questioning, he admitted walking along the New York waterfront with a girl on the day in question. He didn't know her name, and he didn't know whether she was Mary Rogers. He couldn't recall ever having seen a girl of that name. But when he heard about the murder, realising that he had been at the scene, he left town rather than face a lot of awkward questions.

"I didn't kill the girl, whoever she was," he insisted, "and the ferry we were looking for wasn't to Hoboken but to Staten Island. We took the ferry, and when we got to Staten Island I moved my watch back so we would miss the last boat returning. As a result we had to spend the night in a hotel, which was what I intended in the first place."

The police didn't believe a word of this, but then the girl who had accompanied Morse came forward. She did resemble Mary Rogers, and she was hopping mad about Morse's claim that he had seduced her. She wasn't bothered about saving his neck. She had come forward to protest, "He hasn't told all of it. When we went to that Staten Island hotel we took adjoining rooms and I locked the door in between."

Joseph Morse was released, but the story of his attempted infidelity made headlines and he went home to a warm welcome – from his wife's rolling pin.

Now a thorough examination of Mary's corpse revealed that the knot tied in the strip of petticoat which had strangled her was of a type used only by sailors. The hunt began for a sailor who was out carousing that Sunday afternoon and attention became focused on a merchant seaman named William Kukuck. On that Sunday night Kukuck had staggered aboard his ship very late and very drunk shortly before it sailed from New York.

But what the police were particularly interested in was that Kukuck's fellow-seamen remembered there was blood on his trousers.

Kukuck willingly agreed that he had known the beautiful cigar girl on Broadway and said he was actually on his way to see her when he was arrested. Having been away, he had not heard about her murder, nor did he know she was no longer at the tobacconist's shop.

He had spent that Sunday, the day of the murder, in a brothel. The woman proprietor of the brothel confirmed his alibi – she remembered him all too vividly. Her two bouncers had to throw Kukuck out in the early evening when he became obstreperous, and in the process they had each lost a couple of teeth. Kukuck departed with a bloody nose, which accounted for the bloodstains on his trousers.

Two months after the murder, Mrs. Loos, at her Elysian Fields refreshment stall, wanted some wild herbs for a drink she served, so she sent her two small sons into the woods to get them. They returned not only with the herbs, but with three intriguing items they found in a thicket.

These were a silk scarf, a parasol and a handkerchief embroidered with the initials "M.R." The items were handed over to the police who showed them to Mary's mother. She shook her head uncertainly. "They look like Mary's," she said. "But to be honest, I couldn't be sure."

The police couldn't be sure either. Some of them argued that Mrs. Loss may have put the items in the woods to get some publicity, others were convinced that they proved Mary met her death in the thicket.

The same woods were sensationally in the news again only days later, when a hunter making his way along a path near the same thicket found the body of a young man. On the ground nearby was an empty laudanum bottle. Speculation was rife as the body was taken off to the morgue for identification. Here at last, everyone decided, was Mary's killer, and he must have gone to the thicket to commit suicide through remorse.

In the morgue the body was identified – it was that of David Payne. Was he Mary's killer?

At the inquest the coroner dismissed any such suggestion. The empty laudanum bottle, he said, had been in the thicket for at least a year. Payne did not commit suicide, he died from chronic alcoholism. He had not stopped drinking since his fiancée's murder, and although he might have gone to the thicket to grieve, his death there was no more than a coincidence.

So more stories were invented, more speculation dreamed up. But for all the rumours and the theories,

Mary's murder remained unsolved.

One intriguing suggestion caused fingers to point at a woman named Ann Restell, an English-born dressmaker with a profitable sideline as an abortionist at her premises in Greenwich Street. The police learned that Mary was last seen heading in the direction of Greenwich Street, and it was claimed that she could have died as a result of an illegal operation, her apparent strangulation being a cover-up.

If there was any medical evidence to support this idea, it was never made known. But it has to be borne in mind that Ann Restell, having saved many fine reputations from disgrace, was not without influential friends in high places.

Her sideline was nevertheless exposed in 1846 by New York's *National Police Gazette,* to which Edgar Allan Poe was a contributor. Harassed by anti-abortion demonstrators outside her home, Ann Restell committed suicide some years later, leaving an estate worth more than $1 million.

It was also rumoured that old John Anderson, the tobacconist, knew much more about Mary's death than he was prepared to tell. After he died at the age of 80 in 1881, his relatives hinted darkly that he was aware of everything that had happened that fateful Sunday. But when they were questioned by detectives all they could say was that Mary's ghost had appeared to Anderson, "making certain disclosures."

What had the ghost revealed? Anderson's relatives didn't know, because, they said, old John wouldn't talk about it. He regarded all communications from the next world as confidential.

It was left to Edgar Allan Poe, who knew Mary and had bought cigars from the Broadway tobacconist's shop, to develop the literary potential of this intriguing case. His story, *The Mystery of Marie Rogêt,* was first published in a magazine a year after Mary's death. Poe changed the names of Mary, Crommelin and Payne, but they were easily identified by their roles in the enigma, which Poe tried to camouflage by setting the story in Paris.

In this fictionalised version he advanced his own theory of what had happened. The key to the mystery, he believed, lay in Mary Rogers first disappearance. In his story it transpires that Marie – or Mary – spent that absence with her lover, the naval officer later reported to have been seen with a girl resembling the victim. After those seven days of passion in the officer's company she tried to compromise him, so he murdered her, probably on his small boat tied up at the waterfront. Then he dumped her body in the river and set the boat adrift. The story concludes with Poe's detective locating the missing boat, and then tracing its naval officer owner.

This theory takes liberties. No boat featured in the Mary Rogers' investigation. But there must surely have been one, otherwise how did Mary's corpse get into the river? As her body was found floating and had to be towed to the shore, it was almost certainly dumped in midstream.

And whether Poe was right or wrong in his theory, one thing is indisputable. His story made the beautiful cigar shop girl's fate the stuff of legend, and gave her a kind of immortality.

6

CONAN DOYLE

Blueprint for Sherlock Holmes

Dr. Joseph Bell, an Edinburgh surgeon and Professor of Medicine at Edinburgh University, would have been mildly surprised if he knew what was going on in the mind of one of his more studious pupils.

The student, listening avidly to every word the Professor spoke, was Arthur Conan Doyle. What fascinated young Conan Doyle was Professor Bell's remarkable talent for deduction from a patient's appearance and demeanour. Bell could often tell not only what the man was suffering from but also his occupation and where he lived.

Many years later Conan Doyle was to recall how Dr. Bell deduced that a patient had recently been a non-commissioned officer in a Highland regiment stationed in Barbados.

"The man was respectful but did not remove his hat," Bell explained to his students. "Hats are generally not removed in the army, but had he been discharged some time ago he would already have picked up civilian habits. He has an air of authority and is obviously Scottish. As to Barbados, his complaint is elephantiasis, which is West Indian and not British. Elephantiasis is also known as Barbados leg."

Conan Doyle filed away in his memory this example of the professor's deductive ability. Nearly a decade later the young medical student, now qualified as a doctor, created his first story about Sherlock Holmes, and the professor was immortalised as the great detective's model.

"It is most certainly to you that I owe Sherlock Holmes," Conan Doyle told Professor Bell in 1892, five years after the first story was written. And the author subsequently wrote: "It is no wonder that after the study of such a character, I used and amplified his methods when I tried to build up a scientific detective who solved cases on his own merits and not through the folly of the criminal."

The "scientific detective" was to become the most famous of all popular fictional detectives – so famous in fact that even today many people believe there was a real Sherlock Holmes. They have addressed and posted letters to his consulting-room at 221b Baker Street, London, and have tried to find the place for themselves. But neither the detective nor his address were real.

Conan Doyle wrote exactly 60 stories about the great Sherlock, four of them full-length novels, the rest short stories.

The first was *A Study in Scarlet*, a full-length story, published in 1887. This was followed by another long story, *The Sign of Four*, in 1890. Neither book attracted much attention.

But in 1891, when short stories about the detective began to appear regularly in the *Strand Magazine*, both he and his creator were suddenly famous. The stories were later collected in two books.

Just as Holmes often assisted the police (who would have got nowhere without him), so Dr. Bell was often called on by the authorities as a consultant. One of the most dramatic police cases the professor was involved in may have been the trigger that fired Conan Doyle to create Sherlock Holmes.

The case concerned a Frenchman, Eugène Marie Chantrelle, who arrived in Britain in 1862. After teaching French at schools in England, Chantrelle took a job at a private academy in Edinburgh, where he seduced a 15-year-old pupil, Elizabeth Cullen Dyer. When she became pregnant Chantrelle married her in 1868 and in the course of the next few years they had four children.

Then Chantrelle, who was something of a Communist and a revolutionary, began to go off the rails and his teaching career suffered. He lost pupils and income, then started to ill-treat his young wife, bragging that he could kill her and escape detection.

In 1877 he took out a £1,000 policy insuring Elizabeth against accidental death. Not long afterwards a servant found her unconscious in her bedroom. Chantrelle was called to her side, and was left alone with her. A strong smell of gas was noted afterwards, and Chantrelle told the doctor summoned to the scene that Elizabeth had been overcome by gas from a leaking pipe.

It seemed pretty straightforward, and the post-mortem appeared at first to be routine. But the doctor who conducted it was Joseph Bell, whose deductive powers held young Conan Doyle in awe.

Bell decided that Elizabeth Chantrelle had not died of coal-gas poisoning. He suspected a narcotic. The husband was known to have bought opium, which Bell found in traces of Mrs. Chantrelle's vomit on her bed-clothes. This was enough to send Chantrelle to the gallows where, as he was about to be hanged, he scribbled a note which said,

"My compliments to Joseph Bell. He did a good job in bringing me to the scaffold."

Sherlock Holmes owes more to Bell than just the professor's deductive talents. Bell had wide-ranging interests which included the study of handwriting.

His physical appearance certainly calls Holmes to mind. He had a dark complexion, piercing grey eyes, a tall, wiry figure and an odd, jerky gait – and Conan Doyle acknowledged that he had given his famous detective Bell's "eagle face." But Holmes's appearance was also partly based on someone else. The Holmes stories' most popular illustrator was Sidney Paget, and Sidney used his brother Walter, himself an *Illustrated London News* magazine artist, as his model for Holmes.

It was Sidney Paget who endowed the detective with his

famous deerstalker hat. The hat is not mentioned in the stories, but it quickly became an essential part of the detective's image, like his curved pipe, which was added by Sidney Paget's successor, the American illustrator Frederick Dorr Steele.

Dr. Bell's association with the police is believed to have spanned the years 1878 to 1893, concluding with his appearance as an expert witness at the murder trial of Alfred John Monson.

Monson was a private tutor who coached boys for entrance examinations. In 1890 he acquired a new pupil, 17-year-old Cecil Hambrough, the son of Major Hambrough, a landowner who was having some financial difficulties. Monson began to scheme to get his hands on the major's heavily mortgaged estate, which could be sold when Cecil became 18.

With the boy under his influence, Monson tried to manipulate matters to his own advantage. But this did not work out. There were arguments, and Monson and his family moved from Yorkshire to Ardlamont in Argyllshire, taking young Cecil Hambrough with them.

Monson then insured Cecil's life for £20,000, paying the premium with cash acquired through false pretences, and persuading the boy to tell the insurance company that in the event of his death the pay-out should be made to Mrs. Monson.

On Wednesday, August 9th, 1893, Monson took Cecil out in a boat for a day's fishing. There was an "accident" in which the boy nearly – but not quite – drowned. The next day Monson took him out rabbit-shooting, and returned to the house alone. "Mr. Cecil has shot himself," he announced.

Asked by the doctor examining the body if Cecil was insured, Monson replied, "No." The insurance company was suspicious, sent two investigators, and Monson was arrested and charged with murder and attempted murder.

At his trial in December, 1893, it emerged that he had lied about the guns and ammunition used in the shoot. But the defence claimed that he had no murder motive because he would not benefit from Cecil's death. Strictly speaking this was true – the actual beneficiary was Mrs. Monson.

The prosecution's case was based primarily on their plea that Cecil had been shot in a way which ruled out suicide. Their case did not seem too strong until Dr. Joseph Bell stepped into the witness box. When he gave his medical evidence it was in a sense Sherlock Holmes who was speaking. He told how he had examined the victim's skull, studied the post-mortem report, and attended experiments carried out with the two guns taken on the rabbit-shoot. He had also examined the cardboard target and cardboard heads lined with clay which were used in these experiments.

He told the court: "I have been unable to make out any way in which the fatal gunshot could have been done either designedly or accidentally by Mr. Hambrough himself. I have no doubt whatever that the wound was inflicted from behind in a direction almost horizontal, but slightly upwards.

"As regards the distance of the muzzle of the gun from the victim's head when the shot was fired, I have considered the experiments made very carefully and have arrived at the conclusion that the most probable distance was about six to nine feet. Had the wound been inflicted at a lesser distance the skull must have been more smashed up; had the wound been inflicted at a greater distance the body of the shot would have been scattered by the time of impact, and would not have inflicted the deep-grooved wound in the bone which we find has been inflicted.

"My opinion is that this wound must have been inflicted by a gun in the hand of another than the deceased."

So far as is known, this was "Sherlock Holmes's" last real-life case. Despite his evidence, the judge summed up in Monson's favour and the jury returned the Scottish verdict of "Not proven." Curiously, another expert witness who testified at the trial was a Dr. Watson.

Although Dr. Bell was Conan Doyle's principal model for his detective, some of Holmes's attributes have been ascribed to others. His dedication to experimental research may owe something to Professor Sir Robert Christison (1797-1882), an Edinburgh toxicologist who was an expert witness at the trial of the Edinburgh body-snatchers Burke and Hare. In this investigation Sir Robert beat corpses in an attempt to discover if a body would bruise after death.

Holmes's black moods echo those of Conan Doyle's father, an alcoholic artist who ended up in an asylum, and the detective probably owes his manic qualities to Dr. George Turnavine Budd, who was a fellow medical student of Conan Doyle and who later became his partner in a medical practice in Plymouth.

Dr. Budd was a huge man given to violent mood-swings. He was said to have been denied a Rugby international cap only because of his hot temper and contempt for the game's rules. He once told a patient: "Take your medicine, and if that does no good, swallow the cork. There is nothing better when you are sinking." If patients irritated him he threw them out of his surgery. On his premature death in 1889 the post-mortem revealed an abnormality of the brain.

When Conan Doyle himself was asked on whom Holmes was based he named Dr. Joseph Bell, and also acknowledged a debt to Edgar Allan Poe's fictional detective C. Auguste Dupin. But as a freelance investigator Holmes also has a possible prototype in Wendel Scherer, a private detective who had his consulting-rooms in Westbourne Grove, Bayswater, and claimed professional status in a London murder case reported in newspapers four years before Conan Doyle wrote his first Sherlock Holmes story.

In the early draft for that first story the detective is styled "Sherrinford Holmes." The surname is believed to have been borrowed from Oliver Wendell Holmes, a nineteenth-century American author and professor of anatomy whose work Conan Doyle much admired. The choice of

"Sherlock" to replace "Sherrinford" is thought to have come from Conan Doyle's enthusiasm for cricket – Mordecai Sherlock was Yorkshire's wicket-keeper. Holmes, of course, was no cricketer, but he did play the violin, and a well-know violinist of Conan Doyle's day was Alfred Sherlock.

From all these ingredients Conan Doyle fashioned a character who so captures the imagination that Sherlock Holmes' buffs talk about him as if he were flesh and blood. For them he is as real as any Scotland Yard detective – and much more gifted.

Just as Conan Doyle borrowed from real life in creating his detective, so did he model some of his characters on actual criminals. He told G. K. Chesterton, creator of another famous fictional detective, Father Brown, that no writer needed to go further than a classroom or a police station to find a sufficient number of characters to fill any number of novels.

Sherlock Holmes's arch adversary, Professor James Moriarty, styled "The Napoleon of Crime." is modelled upon Adam Worth who, among much else, was responsible for a bank robbery in Boston, Massachusetts, in 1869. This was the genesis of *The Adventure of the Red-Headed League*, in which thieves tunnel their way to a bank's vaults. Worth's exploit was repeated in real life a century later when robbers tunnelled into the vaults of a London bank in 1971. The name "Moriarty" may have been borrowed from George Moriarty, a mentally deranged fellow whose violent, demonic behaviour made headlines when he appeared at Marylebone Magistrates' Court in 1874.

Similarly, Colonel Valentine Walter in *The Adventure of the Bruce-Partington Plans* (*His Last Bow*, 1917) is based on Francis Shackleton, gambler brother of the explorer Ernest Shackleton, who was suspected of involvement in the theft of the Irish crown jewels in 1907.

But it was to Dr. Joseph Bell that Arthur Conan Doyle freely acknowledged he owed his greatest debt, both as the principal inspiration in the creation of Sherlock Holmes and as a friendly mentor at a time when his drunken father was incapable of giving him any guidance, although the artistic Doyle *père* later sobered up sufficiently to draw the illustrations for *A Study in Scarlet*, in which Holmes made his debut.

Conan Doyle dedicated *The Adventures of Sherlock Holmes* to Dr. Bell, who in turn reviewed the book for *The Bookman.* So what did the canny Edinburgh professor think of the stories he had inspired? He wrote that Conan Doyle had "the wit to devise excellent plots and interesting complications." And the tales, he noted, were "absolutely free from padding."

Although Dr. Bell's deductions were the springboard that launched fiction's most celebrated detective, he was better at solving problems than devising them. In his memoirs Conan Doyle recorded: "Bell took a keen interest in these detective tales and even made suggestions which were not, I am bound to say, very practical."

7

DEACON BRODIE

Some laughs with Jekyll and Hyde

William Brodie's privileged background made him a most unlikely criminal. So unlikely that when on two separate occasions two people who knew him caught him in the act of burglary they didn't believe it could be him – and let him get away with it.

Brodie's credentials were copper-bottomed. He was a pillar of society with an unblemished record of public service. Or so I seemed.

For there were two Brodies. By day there was Deacon Brodie the respected city councillor to whom Edinburgh folk deferentially doffed their hats. And by night there was Brodie the cracksman, the prowling criminal everyone feared.

Brodie's double life so fascinated the novelist Robert Louis Stevenson that he used him as the character for his double-imaged *Dr. Jekyll and Mr. Hyde,* a book that added a new compound noun to the English language and made all men familiar with the notion of schizophrenia.

Fiction has persistently pursued the real-life Deacon William Brodie, and much of it has become accepted as fact. As if the true, extraordinary story were not strange enough, his colourful career has become embellished with myths – tall stories the deacon would have relished had he lived to hear them.

The truth was that Brodie was the grandson of two distinguished lawyers, and followed in his father's footsteps to become Edinburgh's leading cabinetmaker and carpenter. In 1763 he became an Edinburgh burgess and in 1781, as Deacon of the Incorporation of Wrights, he was appointed a city councillor, the epitome of respectability.

Far from being the subject of a rags-to-riches story, as he has often been portrayed, he was born into an affluent family – the close in which they lived bore their name – and from his father he was to inherit £10,000 and several houses. Brodie had money, influence, and local respect. Only one thing was missing in his life and he craved it. It was excitement.

There wasn't much of that to be had in his trade as a cabinetmaker or in his role as a town councillor, so Brodie looked around. He discovered that there were thrills a-plenty in cockfighting and gambling, two pastimes which quickly became his twin passions.

Law-abiding Edinburgh citizens went to bed at 10 p.m. Others lived it up at their clubs or low dives like the gambling joint owned by Michael Henderson, where the wealthy and the less-than-wealthy could fritter away their money and possessions. Look for Brodie at two o'clock in the morning and as likely as not you'd find him at Henderson's, gambling with dice and enjoying the cock-fighting, which became such an obsession that he bred his own fighting cocks in his timberyard.

Short, slim and a bit of a dandy, he was already leading something of a double life. His staid fellow-burgesses knew nothing of this and would have been shocked had they known of his nocturnal habits. They were to be dumbfounded by what was to come.

Although his twin gambling passions gave Deacon Brodie a degree of excitement, it wasn't enough. It amused him to think that he was leading a double life, and that the nocturnal one was disreputable and that none of his city colleagues had any inkling of it. But that in itself wasn't sufficient to quench his thirst for real, hair-raising thrills. Nor, more urgently, was it paying for his mounting gambling debts.

And he reasoned, if none of his respectable friends knew about his double life as a gambler, they would never know if he extended it a little further and turned crook.

Brodie began to work on a bold, outrageous plan. In Edinburgh he was trusted and esteemed. His municipal connection brought him most of the corporation's work, and Edinburgh's principal business houses turned to him whenever there was any carpentry to be done.

This meant that he was familiar with their locks, their cupboards and counters, and the location of their safes and strong-boxes. Thanks to his reputation, when his work took him to such places he could move around without ever being questioned. He reckoned that what he didn't know about business houses' security systems, he could soon find out.

So the impeccable Deacon William Brodie became a burglar, carrying out a number of daring raids single-handed. One of his earliest jobs was burgling Johnson and Smith's private bank. A few days before the heist he had been contracted to do some repair work at the bank. The key of the outer door of the premises, he noticed, was kept on a hook in the passageway to the street. He unhooked it, made a quick impression of it in putty, and went home to make his own key.

Several nights later he slipped into the bank using his home-made key, forced the inner door and the door of the safe, and made off with £800 – a considerable sum of money in the late-eighteenth century.

Although he always wore a mask when committing his crimes, on two occasions he was spotted and recognised. The first time his victim was a friend who could not bring himself to confront him and expose him. Brodie even had the effrontery to call the next day and console him on his loss.

On the second occasion he set out to raid the house of an elderly woman who lived alone and who he expected to be out at church that Sunday evening. But she wasn't. She was indisposed and had stayed at home.

She was speechless with amazement as the masked burglar entered the room in which she was sitting, calmly picked up the keys which lay on the table beside her, opened her bureau, removed a large sum of money, re-locked the bureau, replaced the keys on the table and made his exit with a low bow.

"Surely," the old lady said to herself when he had gone, "that was Deacon Brodie!" But she couldn't believe her eyes, and thinking she must have taken leave of her senses she took no action. After all, respectable burgesses didn't go around burgling, did they?

No wonder Brodie thought he could get away with anything. He was now such a successful criminal that he decided to recruit a locksmith as bent as he himself had now become. He found the man he wanted at Michael Henderson's gambling joint.

George Smith was a Birmingham locksmith who was apparently on the run. He had come to Edinburgh from England for reasons he preferred not to talk about, and when Brodie met him at Henderson's he was developing his technique with loaded dice.

Over a drink of ale Brodie proposed a new and profitable future for the Englishman. Smith's eyes glinted. He figured there were big profits in being a respectable burglar, and he wasn't put off by the idea that if he was caught he would be hanged.

His new career was launched with a sideline probably funded by Brodie. Smith became a grocer, a business which gave him a "cover."

Three months after they formed their partnership, the criminal activities of Brodie and Smith were causing waves of alarm in Edinburgh, as big business after big business was burgled cleanly and cunningly, with no clues left by the night-time thieves.

The matter was debated at the city council meeting, where Brodie solemnly held forth on the iniquity of the crime-wave crippling his friends and colleagues. He suggested offering a reward for the thieves' capture and advised his fellow-councillors on security precautions. They listened to him intently, aware of his practical knowledge in such matters.

But if the city councillors had their problems, so did Deacon Brodie. As successful as he had become as a burglar, he still wasn't making enough money to cover his gambling debts. And in addition he had the expense of keeping two mistresses. Anne Grant had already borne him three children, and Jean Watt was the unmarried mother of his two sons.

Brodie and Smith talked about the shortfall in their income and the upshot was that they decided to take on two accomplices: John Brown, a professional burglar, and Andrew Ainslie, who turned out to be good for nothing. He was certainly the world's worst look-out man.

Brown had a criminal history which was later to prove Brodie's undoing. Sentenced in England to seven years' deportation for theft, he had escaped to Scotland. This meant that if he were caught he would be transported – unless he collaborated with the authorities and betrayed his accomplices. Brodie could not have recruited a more dangerous colleague.

Brown's first excursion with his three new companions was to Edinburgh University Library where, in October, 1787, they stole the university's silver mace, selling it to a fence at the Bird in Hand public house in Chesterfield, Derbyshire.

In the following February Deacon Brodie intriguingly fulfilled another role befitting his status as a burgess. Called as a juror in a murder trial in the city courtroom, Edinburgh's ace burglar was empanelled and sat in solemn judgement on the accused. Some time later he was to find himself back in the same court – this time standing in the dock and with his life on the line...

Meanwhile, encouraged by the success of his latest robberies, he selected a more challenging target: the Excise Office in Chessel's Court, Canongate. He was already familiar with the premises, having done work there with his men. Now, on a pretext, he called there with Smith. While Brodie occupied the cashier's attention, Smith made a putty impression of the outer door key which was conveniently hanging from a nail just inside the entrance.

Back at his home Smith made a key which they tested, finding it worked perfectly. But they had noticed that the office had an inner door as well as the outer one, and that beyond that was the door to the cashier's office, which they would have to open. Smith thought this last door would provide a problem.

"We need a really strong cutting tool to force it," he told Brodie. "Something like a plough-coulter." A coulter is a blade or sharp-edged disc attached to a plough so that it cuts through the soil vertically in advance of the ploughshare.

Accompanied by Smith's dog, named Rodney, John Brown and Andrew Ainslie went to Duddington where they spotted a man ploughing. While one of them diverted the ploughman's attention, the other made off with his coulter. The dog Rodney barked and ran about in high glee, thinking it was all a game. But the ploughman was later to remember that dog ...

Ainslie was posted to keep watch on the Excise Office for several nights. He reported that the door-keeper went off duty at eight, and the night watchman did not arrive until ten.

Early in the afternoon of March 4th, 1788, the gang made their final preparations at Smith's home in the Cowgate. The raid was to take place the following night, when they knew that the watchman on duty would be an elderly man. Smith was later to say that Brodie's instructions were that they should grab the watchman and tie him up if he interrupted them. To put him off their trail while he lay helpless listening to them, they would pretend to be smugglers searching for their confiscated loot.

Brodie would also take along a length of rope to be knotted into a ladder, so that if they were taken by surprise they could lock the outer door and escape via the rear windows into the back garden.

During the afternoon of the following day Deacon Brodie entertained guests at his home – his brother-in-law and other relatives, who dropped in for a drink and a chat. He was relaxed, cheerful and seemingly unconcerned about anything. The guests left at 6.30. and half an hour later he joined Smith, Brown and Ainslie at Smith's home, taking with him his pistols, the duplicate key, pick-locks, a chisel and the rope. He also provided a spur. This was to be left at the scene to suggest that the robbery was committed by someone who arrived on horseback. Brown and Smith were armed with pistols, and, as the look-out man, Ainslie was provided with an ivory whistle which Brodie had bought the previous night.

At 8 p.m. Ainslie took up his position in the yard leading to the Excise Office, while Brown tailed the departing door-keeper safely home. Smith and Brown were to force the inner doors and ransack the premises, while Brodie remained in the hall behind the outer door to prevent their being taken by surprise.

Ainslie, hiding behind a wall topped by railings, was to give one blast on his whistle if the watchman appeared, so that the others could pounce and tie him up. If more than one man approached or if there were some other sign of danger, Ainslie was to blow the whistle three times and then go to the Excise Office's back garden to help the others escape by the rear windows.

At first all went well. Smith used a pair of curling-tongs to spring the lock of the inner door and he and Brown then used the coulter to force the door of the cashier's office. To their dismay they could find only £16. They completely overlooked a secret drawer containing £600.

They were still searching when they heard the front door open. They paid no attention to this, assuming that all must be well because there had been no warning from Brodie, in the hall. Then they heard someone hurrying down the stairs and the front door slammed. Realising that something was wrong, they went into the hall. There was no sign of Brodie anywhere, nor was Ainslie at his post outside. Mystified, and cursing the other two men for apparently deserting them, they decided to make a run for it. They made their way to Smith's home, leaving behind the spur, the coulter and two iron wedges.

They were later to learn that not long after Ainslie took up his position, he was startled to see a man run into the yard from the street and into the Excise Office. He was so surprised by this that he didn't blow his whistle, and as the man entered the building another man dashed out. This was Brodie, panicking and fleeing, but in the darkness Ainslie didn't recognise him. Shortly afterwards another figure, taken by Ainslie to be a third man, hurried out of the building and rushed off towards Canongate.

Ainslie now gave three belated blasts on his whistle and dashed round to the back of the Excise Office. But there was no sign of his three companions, so he too decided to make a run for it. He went back to Smith's home where George Smith and John Brown, seething with anger over the fiasco, had already arrived.

The man who had hurried into Excise Office was James Bonar, the Customs' deputy solicitor. Finding the outer door wasn't locked, he had assumed some of the staff were working late and that the man who brushed past him in the hall – Brodie – was one of them. He went upstairs to his office, collected some documents he needed, and – pressed for time – ran downstairs and out of the building, slamming the front door after him.

On hearing him come downstairs Brown and Smith cocked their pistols, but he was gone by the time they stepped out into the hall. If Ainslie had given a single warning blast on his whistle, as arranged, his comrades would have been ready and waiting for the solicitor and would doubtless have shot him. James Bonar owed his life to the fact that both Ainslie and Brodie lost their heads.

Back in the Cowgate, Smith, Brown and Ainslie wondered where Brodie had got to. Unbeknown to them, he too had decided to make a run for it. The deacon rushed home, arriving at about 9 p.m. He changed out of the black clothes he wore for burglary expeditions, put on his normal white attire, and went off to the home of his mistress Jean Watt, where he spent the night to establish an alibi.

Brodie got up early the next morning and went off to meet his three companions. He found them angry and disgruntled, and blaming him for everything that had gone wrong at the Excise Office. Brodie merely laughed.

"We made £16 anyway" he said with a shrug. "Four pounds each." The paltry spoils were divided and the four men went off in their different directions, muttering to themselves.

The most disaffected of them was undoubtedly John Brown. He not only blamed Brodie for the fiasco, but Smith and Ainslie as well. He told himself that he was the only true professional of the four. And then he remembered that a reward of £150 and a free pardon was on offer to whoever could give information leading to the conviction of anyone responsible for the gang's previous raids.

Brown realised that by turning informer he could both collect the reward and free himself from the sentence of transportation hanging over him. This was because the public prosecutor would have to obtain a pardon for him before his evidence could be presented in court.

So with the £4 which was his proceeds of the Excise Office robbery still in his pocket, Brown went to the sheriff's office and spilled the beans. But at this stage he shopped only his fellow partners in crime, George Smith and Andrew Ainslie. He made no mention of Brodie, apparently believing he could make even more money by blackmailing the deacon.

Next day Smith and Ainslie were arrested, and a shocked Deacon Brodie hurried to the jail to see them. This was risky, but he needed to find out how much was known and to induce them to keep quiet about him – if it wasn't too late.

Congratulating the officers at the jail on the burglars' capture, he expressed his curiosity about the pair whose arrest had become the talk of the town and asked to see them. But the jailers' orders were that no one was to have access to the two prisoners, and politely they turned the deacon away. Brodie returned home to consider his next move.

Aware that it could be only a matter of time now before he himself was arrested, he told his foreman the next morning that he was leaving Edinburgh for a day or two on business. Brodie certainly left Edinburgh, but it was not on business. He went to see an influential cousin living outside the city, spilled out the whole story of his double life, and persuaded him – for the sake of the family's honour – to do what he could to help him leave the country.

There is no record of what Brodie's shocked cousin said. But we do know that on that same day, Sunday, March 9th, Brodie boarded a stagecoach for London with a ticket that had been bought for him.

The robbery at the Excise Office was discovered about an hour after he arrived home, and until John Brown split on his companions the only clues the investigators had to go on were the plough-coulter, the spur and the two wedges which the gang had left at the premises. But Brown told the authorities not only about the earlier robbery which carried a reward for information, but also about the raid on the Excise Office. And in doing so he described the theft of the plough-coulter at Duddington.

Smith was taken to the sheriff's office, where he was confronted with the ploughman. Never having seen Smith before, the ploughman didn't recognise him. But he remembered seeing Smith's dog Rodney, with Brown and Ainslie. The dog had followed his master to the sheriff's office, the ploughman recognised the dog and from the fuss Rodney made of Smith it was clear that he was the dog's owner.

Brodie arrived in London on the Wednesday after the

Sunday evening raid to find himself described in the newspapers as a wanted man. There was a £200 reward on offer for his capture. On learning that the deacon had fled, Smith had made a full confession implicating him, and Brodie's involvement was confirmed by Ainslie. Officers searched Brodie's home, found his pistols buried in his timberyard, a bag of false keys, several pick-locks and the lantern he had used on his expeditions.

On Tuesday, March 11th, George Williamson, King's Messenger for Scotland, set out with a court order to find the missing deacon. After drawing a blank at Brodie's local haunts he made inquiries at stage posts along the London Road and learned that the wanted man had boarded a post-chaise at Dunbar on the Sunday afternoon, later transferring at Newcastle to a coach for York and London.

The Newcastle to London coachman remembered the deacon well. He said that on reaching the capital Brodie had alighted in Moorfields, but despite hours of relentless questioning in that area Williamson could find no trace of him. Inquiries made at Dover, Margate and Deal also drew a blank, and the King's Messenger returned to Edinburgh to report that Brodie appeared to have vanished into thin air.

He hadn't, of course. He had taken refuge at the home of a woman friend living near Bow Street. He tried to change his appearance, but could do nothing about the scar under one of his eyes – souvenir of a blow from someone he had cheated at gaming. He also spotted the King's Messenger looking for him, and wrote to tell Michael Henderson: "I saw Mr. Williamson twice, but although countrymen commonly shake hands when they meet far from home, I did not choose to make so free with him notwithstanding he brought a letter to me." The "letter," of course, was a warrant for his arrest.

After reading an unflattering description of himself in a newspaper, Brodie also wrote to Henderson, "I make no doubt but that designing villain John Brown is now in high favour with Mr. Cockburn [the sheriff], for I can see some strokes of his pencil in my portrait. May God forgive him for his crimes and falsehoods."

Through the influence of his cousin in Edinburgh, who pulled strings in London, the deacon sailed for Belgium disguised as an elderly invalid and under the assumed name of John Dixon. The ship was actually bound for Leith, but the Scottish cousin's intermediary – a London lawyer – contrived to have it diverted to Ostend for "Mr. Dixon's" benefit. Bad weather, however, prevented the vessel from putting in to Ostend, and "Dixon" was set ashore at Flushing.

During the voyage he got to know two fellow-passengers, a married couple named Geddes who were returning to Leith, and entrusted them with three letters for delivery to friends in Edinburgh. When the ship arrived in Leith via its journey through Flushing Mr. Geddes caught up with the local news, read Brodie's description in the papers and realised that the letters he carried were written by no less a person than the missing deacon.

They were addressed to Brodie's mistress Anne Grant, his brother-in-law, and to Mr. Henderson. In the letter to his brother-in-law he complained that "my wardrobe is all on my back," and that he had been compelled to flee in old clothes. But he added, "perhaps my cousin judged right that old things were best for my purpose." To Henderson he expressed anxiety for the well-being of his three children by Anne Grant: "May God in His infinite goodness stir up some friendly aid for their support, for it is not in my power at present to give them the smallest assistance. Yet I think they will not absolutely starve in a Christian land, where their father once had friends and who was always liberal to the distressed." He went on to suggest that his eldest daughter – "a fine, sensible girl"– should be apprenticed to a milliner, "but I wish she could learn a little writing and arithmetic first."

Three weeks elapsed before the wayward Mr. Geddes got around to handing the letters to the authorities, but as soon as they realised who had written them they were on

America's great hero,
Charles Lindbergh and
baby Charlie.
Chapter 1

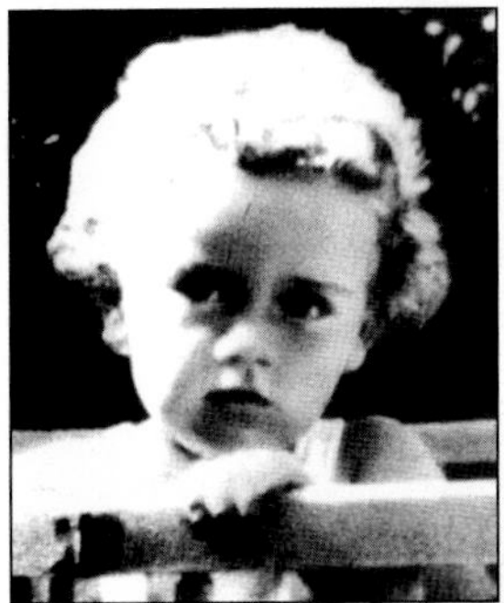

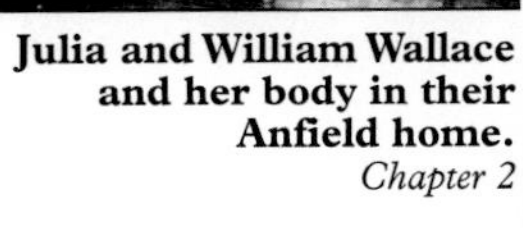

Julia and William Wallace
and her body in their
Anfield home.
Chapter 2

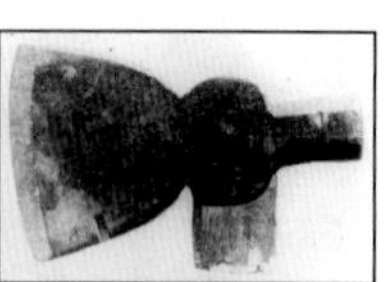

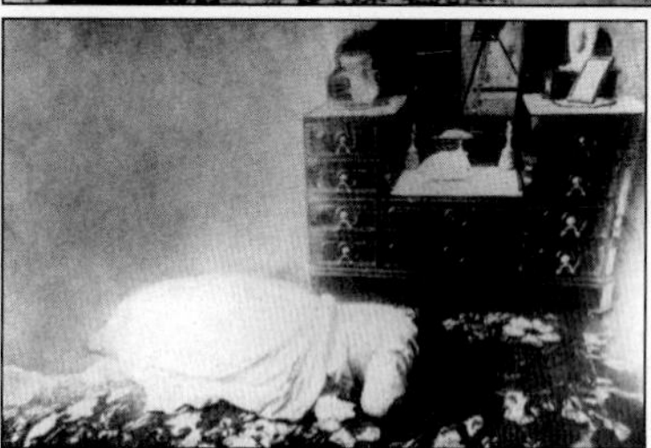

The axe head found in the cellar, the bodies of Mr. and Mrs. Borden, and their daughter Lizzie.
Chapter 3

George Jeffreys. A not so bloody assize.
Chapter 4

Authors Edgar Allan Poe *(Chapter 5)* **and Arthur Conan Doyle.** *Chapter 6*

Dr. Joseph Bell and actor Peter Cushing as Sherlock Holmes.
Chapter 6

The beautiful Viola Kraus, James Elwell at Palm Beach, and reporters and police outside his New York home.
Chapter 8

A Victorian illustration of Sweeney Todd.
Chapter 9

T.E.Lawrence and the motorbike he was killed on.
Chapter 11

Marquis de Sade. He is known as a monster of depravity whose name is perpetuated in the word "sadism"
Chapter 10

Rasputin. Probably the greatest charlatan of the twentieth century.
Chapter 12

Left, Errol Flynn in the guise of Captain Blood and above, Colonel Blood.
Chapter 13

Agatha Christie and the car she abandoned a mile or so from Albury in Surrey.
Chapter 14

Actor Charles Laughton as Captain Bligh and below, an illustration of the famous mariner.
Chapter 15

Jack Kerouac. Caught in a murder mix-up. *Chapter 17*

Maria Manning, the "Bleak House" murderess. *Chapter 16*

Bette Davis in the film *The Letter*, and the real-life victim, William Steward. *Chapter 18*

Brodie's trail again. With the help of the British Consul in Ostend they traced the elusive deacon first to Flushing and ultimately to Amsterdam. There Brodie almost got away, for he was about to sail for America when he was arrested.

He denied he was Brodie, but the evidence of a Scot who had seen him in Edinburgh persuaded the Dutch authorities that the prisoner was undoubtedly the wanted deacon. Brodie was brought to London, where he admitted his identity. His luggage was searched and in it was an unposted letter to a friend in Scotland in which he inquired, "What has been done with the two unfortunate men Smith and Ainslie, and the greater villain John Brown?"

The King's Messenger George Williamson took Brodie back to Edinburgh and afterwards reported that the prisoner was in good spirits on the journey during which "he told many things that had happened to him in Holland." These included meeting a man living on the proceeds of a forgery committed on the Bank of Scotland. As keen as ever to expand his criminal knowledge, the deacon had taken some instruction in forgery from this new acquaintance, and Williamson noted: "Brodie said he was a very ingenious fellow, and had it not been for his own apprehension he would have been master of the forging process in a week."

As they drew near to Edinburgh the deacon, always vain about his appearance, was anxious to shave. Williamson thought twice about entrusting a razor to someone in Brodie's predicament, so he did the job for him. Brodie evidently didn't think much of it. When it was finished the deacon told him: "George, if you're no better at your own business than at shaving, a person may employ you once but I'll be damned if he ever does so again!"

In Edinburgh, meanwhile, John Brown and another of his criminal companions, George White, had been charged with culpable homicide following the death of another man in a drunken brawl. But Brown wasn't worried. He knew his testimony would be vital in the prosecution of Deacon Brodie and he guessed that as a result he would get off. He was right – only George White was sentenced. It seemed that Brown could now literally get away with murder.

George Smith and Andrew Ainslie were still imprisoned in Edinburgh's Tolbooth, but incarceration did not agree with Smith. He converted the iron handle of his lavatory bucket into a pick-lock and made a saw from one of the iron hoops round the bucket. These implements enabled him to take his cell-door off its hinges and go up to Ainslie's cell two floors above, where he picked the lock. He and Ainslie then sawed a hole through the ceiling and the prison's roof, aiming to slide down to the ground by tying their bedsheets together.

They were spotted when some roof slates they disturbed gave way with a clatter. and the two men slid down their makeshift rope straight into the waiting arms of the law. Ainslie subsequently decided to give King's evidence and the charge against him of shopbreaking and theft at the Excise Office was withdrawn, leaving only Brodie and Smith to face the music.

Under 24-hour watch in his Tolbooth cell, the deacon continued to be concerned about his appearance. He was not allowed a knife and fork for his meals, and he wrote indignantly to a fellow-town councillor who was also a magistrate, "The nails of my toes and fingers are not quite as long as Nebuchadnezzar's are said to have been, although long enough for a mandarin and much longer than I find convenient."

He had "tried several experiments to remove this evil," he added. "but without effect. As I intend seeing company abroad in a few days [meaning his trial], I beg as soon as convenient you'll take this matter under consideration... I doubt not but you'll devise some safe and easy method of operation that may give me temporary relief. Perhaps the faculty may prescribe a more radical cure."

He concluded: "If it is not disagreeable to you, I'll be

happy to see you. You'll be sure to find me at home, and all hours are equally convenient."

At first Brodie decided to plead guilty and in his characteristically jocular style drew up a list of the crimes he had intended to go on to commit if he had not been caught. These included stealing the mace from the Council Chamber, breaking into the Bank of Scotland, and holding up the Stirling stagecoach when it was carrying a thousand pounds to pay workmen. His lawyer, however, persuaded him to plead not guilty and for the time being his list of proposed robberies remained a secret.

The Justiciary Court was packed when Brodie and Smith were arraigned on August 7th, 1788, for what was to prove a marathon round-the-clock trial. Troops were called in to line the square outside the court to keep a way clear for the jury and the judiciary. The deacon made his appearance "genteelly dressed in a new dark-blue coat, a fashionable fancy waistcoat, black satin breeches and white silk stockings, a cocked hat, and had his hair fully dressed and powdered," according to a contemporary report. He looked relaxed and confident, whereas Smith, described as "poorly clothed," seemed timid and dejected.

Brodie's defence was led by Henry Erskine, Scotland's leading barrister, and Smith was defended by John Clerk, a little-known but combative junior who, as Lord Eldin in later life, was to say that the trial was the making of him professionally. What he did not say was that the trial also nearly destroyed him professionally. The prosecutors were the Lord Advocate and the Solicitor-General, and the Lord Justice-Clerk, Lord Braxfield, presided, sitting with four other judges.

The trial's most crucial question for both the prosecution and the defence was whether or not Brown and Ainslie should be admitted as witnesses. Apart from the testimony of the two men, the defendants had a good chance of being acquitted, since the evidence against them was mostly circumstantial.

The defence argument was that Ainslie should not be

allowed to testify because he had himself been accused of the crime. The sheriff had promised his life would be spared if he agreed to give evidence against Brodie, about whom he had previously said nothing. Brown's testimony was opposed on the grounds that his pardon preserved him only from punishment and did not expunge his infamy, which rendered him inadmissible as a witness.

When these objections were overruled, the damning testimony of Brown and Ainslie swiftly demolished any prospect of the prisoners being acquitted. The two informers' evidence was further supported by the ploughman who identified the coulter they had stolen, which was found at the scene of the crime. The court also heard how the ploughman had recognised Smith's dog, which had in turn identified its master.

Besides the informers' evidence, the court was asked to accept that Brodie's flight suggested his own guilt, and his letters appeared to be self-incriminating. His alibi had little credibility because his sole witnesses were his mistress Jean Watt and his brother-in-law, neither of whom could be considered impartial.

When John Brown had finished his evidence Lord Braxfield told him, "You appear to be a clever fellow, and I hope you will now abandon your dissipated courses and betake yourself to some honest employment."

"My lord, be assured my future life shall make amends for my past conduct," the villainous informer replied piously.

When the prosecution's case was completed the defence counsel agreed between them that John Clerk should address the court first for Smith, with Erskine following for Brodie. Clerk fortified himself with a bottle of claret and then launched into his attack, saying that Ainslie and Brown should never have been admitted as witnesses.

Lord Braxfield, presiding, appeared scandalised by this impudence from the unknown young lawyer. "Do you say that, sir, after the judgement which the Court has pronounced?" he asked icily. "That, sir, is a most improper observation to address at the outset to the jury."

Lord Braxfield's fellow-judges agreed. "It is a positive reflection on the court," said Lord Stonefield. And Lord Hailes protested: "It is a flat accusation that we have admitted improper evidence." Lord Eskgrove weighed in: "I never heard the like of this from any young counsel at the beginning of his career at this bar." Only Lord Swinton remained silent.

"With these admonitions, go on, sir; proceed, sir," said Lord Braxfield.

"I am awed, my lords. If I go on, I beg to assail at the outset the evidence of these two corbies or infernal scoundrels, Ainslie and Brown," Clerk continued.

"Take care, sir, what you say," warned Lord Braxfield.

To applause from the spectators, Clerk proceeded, taking no care at all to avoid treading on the judges' corns. As he again claimed that Ainslie and Brown should not have been admitted as witnesses, Lord Braxfield told him, "This is most indecent behaviour. You cannot be allowed to speak to the admissibility; to the credibility, you may."

"This young man is again attacking the court!" Lord Stonefield protested.

But Clerk was unabashed. When he claimed that "the jury are to judge of the law as well as the facts," Lord Hailes could not contain himself. "Sir," he cried, "do you deny the authority of this High Court?"

And when Lord Braxfield told Clerk, "You are talking nonsense, sir," the young counsel warned him, "My lord, you had better not snub me in this way. I never mean to speak nonsense."

"Gang on, sir," Lord Braxfield replied wearily.

And Clerk did just that. When the prosecutor reminded him that Brown had received "His Majesty's free pardon," Clerk – to further applause – asked, "Can His Majesty make a tainted scoundrel an honest man?"

"The prerogative of mercy is the brightest jewel in His Majesty's crown" replied the Lord Advocate, one of the prosecutors.

"I hope His Majesty's crown will never be contaminated by any villains around it," Clerk responded.

"Do you want his words noted down?" Lord Braxfield asked the Lord Advocate.

"Oh, no, my lord, not exactly yet," the prosecutor replied. "My young friend will soon cool in his effervescence for his client."

But John Clerk did not cool. He became even more fiery. When he once more told the jury that they were the judges of both the law and the facts, Lord Braxfield cried: "We cannot tolerate this, sir! It is an indignity to the High Court – a very gross indignity deserving of the severest reprobation!"

"Unless I am allowed to speak to the jury in this manner, I am determined not to speak a word more," Clerk countered and sat down.

"Go on, sir," Lord Braxfield urged even more wearily. "Go on to the length of your tether."

Rising again, Clerk repeated to the jury, "You are the judges of the law as well as of the facts."

"Beware of what you are about, sir," cautioned Lord Braxfield. "Go on at your peril."

But Clerk refused to proceed unless he was allowed to say what he was determined to say without interruption or threat. Lord Braxfield then invited Erskine to begin his speech for Brodie, but shaking his head, Erskine declined to do so. Then as Lord Braxfield turned to address the jury with his summing-up, Clerk sprang to his feet, shook his fist at the bench and cried, "Hang my client if ye daur, my lord, without hearing me in his defence!"

There was a stunned silence. Then the judges retired to consult each other.

What would happen when they returned? Would the impertinent young John Clerk be arraigned for contempt? To everyone's surprise, when the judges resumed their seats they invited him to continue. Undeterred, Clerk rose and addressing the jury, scoffed at the testimony of Brown and Ainslie as "good for nothing."

By the time Erskine rose to the address the jury on behalf of Deacon Brodie, it was three o'clock in the morning. The trial had begun at 9 a.m. the previous day, but Erskine showed no sign of exhaustion as he made the most of what little he could say for his client.

Lord Braxfield began his summing-up at 4.30 a.m., concluding hour-and-a-half later when the court adjourned until 1 p.m. The jury and the two prisoners had been in their seats for nearly 24 hours.

"Mr. Brodie's behaviour during the whole trial was perfectly collected," the *Edinburgh Advertiser* reported. "He was perfectly respectful to the court, and when anything ludicrous occurred in the evidence he smiled as if he had been an indifferent spectator."

How long did the jury sleep during the seven-hour adjournment, and how long was left for deliberation? We shall never know. But they apparently had no trouble reaching the verdict they delivered as soon as the court reassembled. They found both Brodie and Smith guilty.

As the two men were sentenced to death Brodie appeared about to speak, but was restrained by his counsel. Instead, he contented himself with bowing to the bench. Smith's solicitor later commented that while his client appeared dejected, "Mr. Brodie affected coolness and determination in his behaviour. It is said that he accused his companion of pusillanimity, and even kicked him as they were leaving the court."

The two men now had to share the condemned cell with two other men who had been sentenced to death for robbing a Dundee bank. Each was chained by one foot to an iron bar, but Brodie's chain was reported to be longer than the rest, enabling him to sit at a table and write.

To pass the time he scratched a draughtboard on the stone floor, playing with anyone who would join him, and when he had no contestant he matched his right hand against his left. The draughtboard remained inscribed on the cell's floor until the prison's demolition nearly 30 years later.

Appeals to have Brodie's death sentence commuted to transportation for life were unsuccessful, but he continued to maintain a brave front and broke down only once – when his eldest daughter visited him shortly before his execution, which he wryly described as his "leap in the dark."

Brodie even had a word to say about the noise made by the workmen assembling the scaffold. He considered "their racket sounded like that made by shipbuilders, but for the short voyage I am to make I think so much preparation unnecessary."

On the appointed day, October 1st, 1788, he was coolness itself. The largest crowd ever seen in Edinburgh assembled to watch him make his exit, and Deacon Brodie rose to the occasion by appearing "in a handsome suit of black clothes, his hair powdered and dressed with taste."

There were two delays, the hangman twice finding that his rope was improperly adjusted. Each time Brodie descended from the platform to chat with his friends. Apologising for the delays, he explained that the apparatus was a new construction and required only a little more practice to make it work perfectly. And when one of the spectators offered condolences on his sad fate, he replied: "What would you have? It is the fortune of war."

When the hangman was at last satisfied that all was ready, the deacon once more briskly mounted the ladder, shook hands with his partner in crime George Smith, untied his cravat and helped the executioner fix the rope. Then he put on the white night-cap handed to him, and seconds later it was all over.

But not for some. Deacon Brodie had been such a colourful character that many did not wish to part with him and could not bring themselves to believe he was dead. Or so it seems, for it was at this point that legend took over from reality.

Dead though Deacon Brodie doubtless was – his neck was adjudged to be broken by the hanging – the rumourmongers refused to let him lie down. It was claimed that when his friends found that he was too well-guarded to be rescued, they arranged for him to ask to see one or two of them alone shortly before his execution. This request was granted, and a specially-made silver tube was slipped down his throat to prevent strangulation, wires being hidden under his clothes from head to foot to preserve him from the jerk of the rope. These preparations, it was said, explained the deacon's remarkable coolness at his execution.

Describing the "plot" further, the myth-makers claimed that the hangman was persuaded to give Brodie a short drop, a surgeon bled him as soon as he was cut down, and he then feigned death as he lay in his coffin until it was safely handed over to his relatives for interment.

The sequel to this, they said, was that Deacon Brodie escaped from Scotland, was later seen and spoken with in Paris, and when his grave was opened it was found to be empty.

Another account of his last hours said that on the day before his execution Brodie was visited in prison by a French quack, Dr. Peter Degravers – who was indeed then in Edinburgh, advertising his services at half-a-crown a consultation. Degravers was said to have offered to bring the deacon back to life after his hanging, and to have marked the condemned man's arms and temples with a pencil so that he would know where to apply his lancet as soon as he had access to the body.

But the hangman, having been bribed to give the deacon a short drop, miscalculated and gave him too long a fall, with fatal consequences. So when two of Brodie's workmen collected the body, placed it in a cart and set off at a gallop, the hanged man really was quite dead. And when the body was delivered at one of Brodie's own workshops for Degravers's attention, the Frenchman's efforts to restore life were unavailing.

That account was written nearly a hundred years after the deacon went to the scaffold. And by then the romancers had also turned their attention to the gallows, claiming that Brodie had himself designed and built the apparatus which despatched him, and that he was its first victim.

It is possible that the deacon prepared a model for the gallows – based on improvements recently introduced in England – but the records of Edinburgh Corporation show that the contract went to another carpenter who had replaced Brodie on the town council. And as this scaffold was built two years before the execution of Deacon Brodie and George Smith, it is unlikely that they were its first customers.

True to form, a few days before his execution Brodie peppered his last will and testament with jokes. His property having been confiscated by the Crown, he noted that he had "nothing else to dispose of but my good and bad qualifications."

To a chimney-sweep who had sued him for cheating at gambling he bequeathed "my dexterity in cards and dice, which may enable him to refund himself of the five guineas, two half-guineas and six shillings which he prosecuted me for." To another acquaintance he left "my sobriety and good breeding, which may save him from being kicked out of company."

And to "my good friends and old companions John Brown and Andrew Ainslie" he bequeathed "all my bad qualities, not doubting, however, but their own will secure them a rope at last."

f

8

JAMES ELWELL

Who killed the society celebrity?

At 25 James Bowne Elwell was burning with ambition, but he was still only a hardware salesman. Things could only improve. And they did.

For from his schooldays Elwell was a wizard at cards. Bridge attracted him, he mastered it, and by the time he was 45 he had grown wealthy from the game.

He played for high stakes at Brooklyn's Irving Republican Club and his success prompted fellow-members to ask him for lessons. He became such a good tutor that teaching was soon his sole occupation. He turned his lessons into books, ghost-written by his wife, which became best-sellers.

As more and more wealthy New Yorkers sought him out, his sphere of operations moved from Brooklyn to glitzy Fifth Avenue. As his career flourished and his income soared, his family life became a drag. In 1916, after twelve years of marriage, he separated from his wife, paying her $200 a month and financing their son's education. Then he moved into a three-storey luxury bachelor pad of his own at 244 West Seventeenth Street.

There seemed no heights that Elwell could not scale. His big winnings at cards, backed up by a successful venture into cotton-trading and $20,000 a year royalties from his books, enabled him to buy racehorses and build a new home for his parents.

He was now a popular man-about-town, well known in New York society, always at the right places with the right people. Softly spoken, amiable and noted for his poise, he was at ease in all classes of society. He had become an accomplished golfer and tennis player as well as a brilliant bridge player. Acquaintances noted that his interest in games of chance was philosophical and experimental rather than nurtured by a desire for money.

Joseph Elwell also liked women, and they liked him. A succession of beauties passed through his bachelor pad and his other houses at Palm Beach, Long Beach and Saratoga Springs. More than 150 women were listed in his address book. Photographs of 90 of them were found at his home, and he was paying regular allowances to 14 of them.

In the early hours of the morning of Friday, June 11th, 1920, Elwell returned from a night club to his New York home. He needed to catch up on some sleep, for that afternoon he was due to go off on a weekend party. He never made the party, and the events of that night indicated that he didn't have much time to catch up on his sleep either. At one stage he sat in a chair and read a letter. As he looked up he stared into the eyes of his killer. A shot was fired and Elwell slumped, dying.

Was he shot by a jilted mistress, a jealous husband or some enraged brother? Or was the murder motive to be found elsewhere – in a racetrack dispute, a card swindle or perhaps blackmail?

The police learned that 12 hours before his death Elwell had dined at the Ritz-Carlton restaurant. His dinner companions were Walter Lewisohn and his wife Selma, wealthy socialites, and Mrs. Lewisohn's beautiful young sister Viola Kraus.

During the meal there was a momentary embarrassment. Two tables away were Victor Von Schlegell, a former Yale football star, and Miss Emily Anderson. Earlier that same day Von Schlegell had obtained a final divorce decree from Viola Kraus, from whom he had been separated for some months.

Both parties, however, seemed perfectly at ease. Later that evening, Elwell and his dinner companions went to a night club, the Midnight Frolic, where they met a journalist friend and invited him to join their table. They were telling him of their odd encounter with Von Schlegell and Emily Anderson, whom the journalist knew, when Von Schlegell walked in and sat down just two tables away from them.

There were smiles, and some looks of astonishment, all round at this remarkable coincidence. But when Von Schlegell called across some pleasantry, Elwell seemed suddenly irritated.

Von Schlegell and Miss Anderson left the night club early. After that Elwell and Viola Kraus were involved in a mild tiff. They left the night club at 2 a.m. Outside, on Forty-Second Street, Elwell was invited to ride with the Lewisohn party, but he seemed put out. He replied petulantly that the cab would be too crowded, doffed his hat and began walking west along Forty-Second Street.

He had walked no more than half a block when he picked up a cab. He was driven north to Sixty-Sixth Street, where he told the driver to pull in at the nearest newsstand. He got out, bought a *Morning Telegraph*, and returned to the cab.

Arriving home, he paid the driver and gave him a tip. As the driver took out his log book to record the trip, Elwell walked up the three steps to his front door. He turned and glanced back at the cab while getting out his keys. The driver noted the time as Elwell disappeared through the door – it was 2.30 a.m.

Within half an hour Viola Kraus phoned Elwell to patch up their quarrel. Where she called from the police never disclosed. The phone company's records showed that at 4.39 a.m. Elwell tried to call his horse-racing partner, W. H. Pendleton, with whom he jointly owned a large stable. The operator rang Pendleton's number for several minutes, but there was no reply. Pendleton later told detectives that his bedside phone never rang – and he added that at no time in his three-year association with Elwell had his partner ever phoned him at night.

At 6.09 a.m. Elwell called another number, on the Garden City, New York, exchange. Whether he was connected, and who he was phoning, was never revealed.

The phone company's records indicated that two attempts had been made to reach numbers from Elwell's home about an hour before his return, but the times of these two calls had not been logged by the operators. They thought the calls were made at around 1.30 a.m.

At 6.15 a.m. a milkman made a delivery at Elwell's home. At 7.10 a postman opened the outer front door, left some letters on the tiled floor, and pressed the bell twice as usual.

Mrs. Marie Larsen, Elwell's housekeeper, who had the only other key beside Elwell's to the new lock installed on the front door, arrived shortly afterwards. She picked up the milk, unlocked the door and went in. She was passing the living room when she noticed some letters strewn on the floor. She went into the room, picked them up, and as she did so she saw Elwell's bare feet. Looking up, she saw that he was slumped in his chair, shot between his eyes. Blood spattered the wall, his face, the chair and the carpet. He was breathing laboriously, and for a moment she did not recognise him.

She stumbled, fell, and then ran from the house to the milkman, who was making deliveries to other houses.

"Mr. Elwell has been killed!" she cried. "Call a doctor!"

The milkman said they must fetch a policeman, so they ran in opposite directions to find one. Officer Henry Singer responded, and Elwell was taken to Bellevue Hospital where he died within an hour without regaining consciousness.

Mrs. Larsen said that at first she thought her employer had shot a burglar. She could hardly recognise him because he was bald-headed and had no teeth, and she had never seen him like that before. With his toupee off and his teeth out, he had obviously not been expecting company.

District Attorney Edward Swann, Captain Arthur Carey of the Homicide Bureau and Medical Examiner Dr. Charles Norris were soon at the scene.

The house had three entrances: the front door, a small door under the street stairs giving access to the basement, and a rear door. All the doors and windows had been locked from the inside except a single window in Elwell's bedroom on the second floor, left open for ventilation. Heavy iron bars covered most of the ground floor windows.

The investigators believed that unless Elwell had admitted someone or had carelessly left the front door ajar, no entrance could have been made after he arrived home. But it was possible that the killer had been hiding in the house for some hours.

Although Elwell had not gone to bed, a single dented pillow indicated that he had lain there reading the *Morning Telegraph*, which lay on the floor beside his bed. At the foot of the bed his clothes were neatly folded on a chair. They contained about $400. His jewellery, valued at about $7,000, was undisturbed on the dresser, beside his false teeth and toupee. The only signs of violence or intrusion were in the blood-spattered living room.

The chair in which Elwell was found was facing the fireplace and was positioned near the door to the hall. The only object on a small table to his right was a steel-jacketed .45 calibre bullet. It had passed through his head, hitting the wall behind and above him before it landed on the table.

The killer had apparently been nervous and hurried – otherwise he or she would have removed the tell-tale bullet, which had been fired from an automatic pistol. He or she could have hidden behind another chair in the room, but the shot had been fired from directly in front of the victim.

The investigators believed that the killer must have been seated when the gun was discharged. They thought that Elwell – probably having asked his visitor to sit down and talk things over – had been fully aware that he was facing death and had exercised his poker-playing nerve to control the situation.

When Mrs. Larsen discovered the body she noticed that the second chair was in the centre of the floor, instead of in its usual position. It had evidently been moved sideways a few inches as the killer rose from it after the shooting. Detective Harry Butts, the police department's ballistics expert, thought the chair had been directly opposite Elwell while the killer occupied it.

The room also contained a card table. There were three valuable paintings on the walls, and a plain wooden frame containing Rudyard Kipling's poem *If*. A cheap cigarette, not at all the type Elwell smoked, was found on the living room mantelpiece. The phone was on a table near the window...but something was wrong with it – a policeman had to run next-door to call headquarters. Mrs. Larsen said the phone had been out of order – yet Viola Kraus had called and spoken to Elwell, and the phone company's records also showed that other calls had been made from the house.

The police decided that the killer's presence must have been unknown to Elwell until a moment prior to the shooting, or else Elwell never expected violence from his visitor.

If the killer were a supposed friend, who could this be? Elwell was certainly canny enough to avoid having anyone who might threaten him in the house at that hour. So was his visitor a relative? That seemed possible, for who but a relation would be permitted to see him bare-footed and without his teeth and toupee?

The police learned that Elwell had been particularly kind to his parents. His brother and two sisters had cast-iron alibis, and so did his estranged wife Helen. She did not care for his mode of life and had ceased to be interested in him. He had made a fortune from the books she had ghost-written, and then he had left her. She felt he was less than generous in the financial support he continued to give her. Was that a motive for murder?

The letter Elwell had been reading had dropped to his lap when he was shot. It was from his racing trainer at Covington, Kentucky, and nothing in it or in his unopened mail offered any clue to the mystery. The police questioned every man and woman whose name or picture was found at Elwell's home. All could prove alibis for the time of the murder.

From the outset there was immediate interest in Viola Kraus, but for several weeks she was known to the Press only as "Miss Wilson." The district attorney had decided to keep her identity secret, saying, "I will not pander to the morbid taste of scandal-mongers."

When he finally reluctantly identified "Miss Wilson" as Miss Kraus, he said: "The young woman is in an unfortunate position. There is no inclination to disclose her frailties. If she was the cause of a criminal act we have no conclusive proof of it. I am unwilling to render more miserable in this case the wretched lot of young women who have stooped to folly. Nor will I parade frailties until guilt is established in connection with the murder."

Some pink lingerie and a pair of pink bedroom slippers were found in the room adjoining Elwell's, and Mrs. Larsen said they were Viola's. But the housekeeper had never seen any of Elwell's women callers, and knew none of their names. She had only heard their voices.

When the identity of "Miss Wilson" eventually became known, Viola Kraus and her sister Mrs. Lewisohn were besieged by reporters. The sisters said they first met Elwell eight years earlier at Palm Beach. Thereafter they saw him about a dozen times a year, but more frequently after Viola's split from Victor Von Schlegell the previous September.

The sisters said that Elwell knew Von Schlegell before his marriage to Viola. Von Schlegell had been friendly towards Elwell throughout the five-year marriage. The sisters knew that Elwell was not divorced from his wife, and they insisted that there had been no suggestion that he would obtain a divorce and remarry.

Viola said that although she enjoyed socialising with Elwell, he had no attraction for her as a suitor. Her story was supported by Von Schlegell, who said he had never been jealous of Elwell.

The murder victim was to have been the sisters' guest over the weekend. Unaware of the shooting, on the morning of his death Viola phoned his home to make arrangements. The phone was now working again, and the call was answered by a detective who said that Elwell was ill and she was needed at his home. The sisters arrived to find themselves surrounded by newspaper photographers.

In a subsequent interview redolent with a 1920s society lady's dismay at the indignity of being questioned about a murder, Viola Kraus told reporters: "Mr. Elwell was to have gone with my sister Mrs. Lewisohn and myself to her home in New Jersey to play golf on Friday afternoon and Saturday. It was to have been a small house-party and we intended to start around two o'clock Friday afternoon in the motor.

"The night before, just before we left him at the Midnight Frolic, he asked us to call him up and tell him when he should be ready, so on Friday around noon I telephoned his house to say we would call by for him about half-past two. A man's voice answered the telephone [this was the detective] and when I asked for Mr. Elwell he asked me if I was a friend of his, which of course I said I was.

"I said, 'What's the matter?' The man told me to come over at once. My sister, Mrs. Lewisohn, was then at my mother's house. I phoned her at once and she said she would meet me at Mr. Elwell's house right away.

"We didn't know what we could do, but we felt it was the least we could do since we were his friends and had been out with him just the night before, and evidently he needed such help as we might be able to give him.

"I have only a confused idea of what I thought, but it occurred to me we might be able to telephone doctors or nurses, or make hospital arrangements. I reached the house around one or two o'clock. The detectives asked me all sorts of questions. I was completely overwrought by the whole thing. Mrs. Lewisohn came in just a few minutes later, and they questioned her in the same terrible and embarrassing way.

"If it hadn't been for my telephone call to the house I shouldn't have gone there, and then we wouldn't have been subjected to this fearfully unpleasant notoriety. I don't suppose I'd been at Mr Elwell's house more than twice before in my life. I stopped by there once to pick him up when I was in the motor with my brother, and one other time around last Christmas when he was sick, I stopped by and sent the chauffeur in with some books and magazines.

"I always thought Mr. Elwell was a nice fellow, but he did not have the least attraction for me sentimentally. I never found in him the attraction for women the newspapers say he had.

"Von knew him before we were married, and after that when we had a cottage down on Long Island. Mr. Elwell would come down occasionally and golf with us, but in the entire time I don't believe that he ever was in any way more attentive to me than he was to other women, and certainly not in any way that caused even the slightest comment from Von or anybody else.

"But even if he had been, my own attitude toward him was one of such complete indifference, except as to his being a pleasant companion, as to remove such a thought.

"I knew that Mr. Elwell, while living apart from his wife, was not legally separated. I knew and my sister knew it and Von knew it; everybody knew it. He never made a secret of the fact that he wasn't divorced. We knew him to be a married man living his own life, and we naturally thought his wife was too. He referred to her rarely, and when he did it was always in pleasant terms, and we thought the estrangement was due to incompatibility.

"That was the case with me. After not quite four years of our marriage Mr. Von Schlegell and I found we weren't getting along together very well, and so we separated finally last September. My marital experience was not one that would tempt me to try it again, and our separation wasn't in any way due to any question of another man."

The couple's friends agreed that Von Schlegell had never been jealous of his wife. He preferred the freedom of a single life and having gained that, the two had remained friends.

Viola Kraus added: "It was the merest chance that my ex-husband happened to be at the Ritz-Carlton when we were there Thursday night. I did not know who Mr. Von Schlegell's companion was, but he knew everybody at our table and his greetings to all of us were cordial.

"Until I saw the intimations in the paper, thinly veiled, I hadn't the slightest idea they wanted to question Mr. Von Schlegell. I knew nothing of his movements beyond what I have read in the papers, just as I have known nothing of his life since our separation.

"The detective and the district attorney have told us that they have no further questions to ask, but insinuations and innuendoes of a most terrible sort still continue. If we can say or do anything that will stop the use of our names any further in this awful thing we shall be happy, and that is why we are consenting to an interview. We want the mystery to be cleared up so that whoever is guilty will be punished, but we have almost as great a reason for wishing it from the fact that it will stop the use of our names."

Victor Von Schlegell's companion, Emily Anderson, had returned to her home in Minneapolis the morning following the Ritz-Carlton and Midnight Frolic encounters, catching a train about three hours after Elwell was shot. Recalled to New York, she told detectives: "Mr. Von Schlegell phoned me on Wednesday. Learning that I intended going home Friday, he invited me to dinner Thursday evening, giving me my choice of any restaurant in New York. I chose the Ritz-Carlton because it was the most fashionable, and felt that as it was to be my last party in New York I would make it a nice one.

"We met Mr. Elwell twice in the course of the evening. Both meetings were casual and brief and apparently without any ill feelings on either side. Miss Viola Kraus, Mr. Von Schlegell's divorced wife, was with Mr. Elwell on both occasions. When we reached our table at the Midnight Frolic we found we were only two tables away from the Elwell party.

"As we sat down Mr. Von Schlegell remarked with a laugh that he seemed unable to keep away from Viola Kraus even though the law had given him the privilege. Miss Kraus had just received her divorce decree. Of course the remark was a joke, and when he spoke to me at other times about Miss Kraus it was always with the kindest feelings.

"We later took a cab to my apartment on East Sixty-First Street, and Mr. Von Schlegell said goodnight. He did not come in with me. He said something about going home. I went to bed and the next morning I went down to Grand Central Station to take my train home, and I was astonished to hear the newsboys crying out, 'All about the Elwell murder!'"

Questioned further, however, Emily Anderson admitted she had lied. She'd spent the night and had breakfast with Von Schlegell – who she was later to marry – before catching her train home.

Von Schlegell, an executive of the United Rubber Manufacturing Company, admitted that he owned "a large army pistol", but its calibre was not that of the murder weapon. His breakfast with Emily Anderson made his presence at the crime scene virtually impossible – unless both were lying.

It subsequently emerged that in the last week of May, 1920, Elwell had written what was only his second letter to his wife since their separation. In this he asked her for a divorce. He had spent the following weekend with Viola and the Lewisohns. Viola's divorce was to be completed within a few days, and it seemed probable that Elwell would have told his friends that he too was seeking a divorce.

Walter Lewisohn, the husband of Mrs. Selma Lewisohn, became a suspect when it was learned that he had become infatuated with Leonora Hughes, a beautiful dancer in whom Elwell was also interested. Did this give Lewisohn a motive for murder? Leonora had frequently been seen in the Lewisohns' company, so why wasn't she in the Ritz-Carlton party that fateful evening? Was Lewisohn keeping her away from the divorce-seeking, predatory bridge-player?

The police also learned of a curious incident that had occurred on the Sunday night prior to the murder, when Elwell's chauffeur was driving him home from the Lewisohns' mansion. Although the car had recently been serviced, a wheel came off and they were lucky to escape injury. Elwell, mentioning this to friends, had said he sometimes feared for his life because of his war-time activities against enemy aliens. He didn't elaborate, and nobody knew what he meant.

Detectives took Viola Kraus's story with a pinch of salt. They believed she had been closer to Elwell than she would admit, and it was learned that she considered another woman, Mrs. Josephine Wilmerding, of New York, to be her rival for his affections. Mrs. Wilmerding, a divorcee, said she knew nothing of Elwell's affairs except that "Miss Kraus was playing around with him."

At this point the police contacted Elwell's former maid Anna Kane, who had returned to Ireland. In a cabled response she said she had heard Viola Kraus quarrelling with Elwell over another woman, threatening him if he dared to desert her.

Elwell's wife said that although he had abandoned her for younger women, he was principally interested in their money. She challenged reports that a number of women had keys to her husband's home. "He never cared for any one woman long enough to let her have a key, I am quite sure," she said.

Acquaintances had often heard Elwell say that women

should be chloroformed after they were 30.

The shooting was believed to have taken place in the hour before 8.10 a.m. So detectives wondered how the killer had managed to exit from the front door unnoticed at a time when servants were stirring in the neighbourhood and pedestrians were passing. Everyone on the block and everyone who used Seventeenth Street as their route to work was interviewed, but none had seen anyone leave Elwell's home during the time in question.

The victim's friends said that on coming face to face with a gun he would have shown no fear. They believed he would have confronted his visitor in a bored, inattentive manner, even perhaps opening and reading a letter while his life was being threatened, as if oblivious to his caller's presence. They insisted that he would not have condescended to promise, plea or argue, even though he knew that his next moment could be his last.

The district attorney was convinced that the killer could not have entered the house before Elwell's return. According to the locksmith who had altered the front door lock a few months before the shooting, there were only two keys. So none of the old keys Elwell was said to have given to various women could have been used by the killer.

While the murder remained unsolved, the various participants in the drama went on to have mixed fortunes. Walter Lewisohn's was the worst. His increasing obsession with Leonora Hughes led to his confinement in an asylum. He spent the next ten years there, talking to her on a dummy telephone.

Viola Kraus changed her name to Cross, opened a millinery business in Paris and subsequently became a fashion model. Elwell's widow succeeded in getting part of his estate for their son. Most of the estate, however, went to Elwell's parents.

The mystery tantalised the public, many of whom had their own pet theories. And it intrigued Willard Huntington Wright, a sophisticated and scholarly New York journalist who had become the first American magazine editor to publish the works of D.H. Lawrence and James Joyce. Afflicted in 1925 by an illness which prevented him from continuing in his profession, he adopted the pen-name S.S. Van Dine and turned his hand to detective fiction.

His first novel, based on the murder of Elwell, featured Philo Vance – an American Lord Peter Wimsey – exposing the killer of Alvin Benson, who was instantly recognisable as Joseph Elwell.

"The whole book has that professional air about it which makes one feel the crime really happened and that one is not reading a piece of pure fiction," says the editor's introduction to Van Dine's *The Benson Murder Case*, published in 1926. Well, of course the crime really did happen. But the end was somewhat different – New York police failed to solve the case of Joseph Elwell, while Van Dine came up with a solution in his novel.

It became a best-seller, and was followed by 11 more novels in which Philo Vance cracked further cases. On the screen he was portrayed by the film star William Powell.

In life Elwell had made a fortune from his books. His death made another author's fortune. But his murder remains the enigma it was the day his housekeeper looked up from the strewn letters, to see he was not as handsome as she had thought.

9

SWEENEY TODD
Fact or fiction?

Sweeney Todd - was he fact or fiction? Did he really exist, or was he the creation of Victorian "penny dreadfuls"?

Many writers have claimed in the past that the "Demon Barber of Fleet Street" who reportedly cut his victims' throats and turned their bodies into meat pies, was not a real person. "As a matter of fact, no absolute record of such a personage or crime exists in criminal annals," says one source. "A belief that Sweeney Todd was executed at Tyburn long prevailed, but it is apparently unfounded."

Todd's detractors point to the fact that his name does not appear in any list of executions such as *Hayd's Dictionary of Dates,* published in 1895 or *The Complete Newgate Calendar,* published by the Navarre Society. Surely some reference would have been made of such an illustrious mass murderer.

Nevertheless, Sweeney Todd stories have abounded across two centuries. Nor was he the only demon barber, from all accounts. A writer, J. L. Smith, mentions five notorious women barbers operating in Drury Lane, in his book *The Ancient Topography of London.* They committed "shameful crimes" including robbing their victims, and lived on in ballad form:

Did you ever hear the like
Or ever hear the same,
Of five women barbers
Who lived in Drury Lane.

The first Sweeney Todd melodrama opened at London's

Britannia Theatre in 1842, and was revived on many occasions, up to as late as 1878. In the 1970s a new Sweeney Todd musical played in London and on Broadway, where it starred Angela Lansbury. Most of the audiences would never have guessed that the basis of the horrific tale was anything else than a myth.

But in 1973 the author Peter Haining published *Sweeney Todd*, a study claiming that the murderous British barber was flesh and blood, and every bit as demonic as the legendary villain he became in countless melodramas.

Haining quotes from a leading article in an issue of the *Daily Courant*, published at around Christmas, 1801.

"Scarcely ever in London has such an amount of public excitement been produced by any criminal proceedings as by the trial of Sweeney Todd," exclaims that newspaper. "The most hideous crimes have been laid to his charge, and in the imagination of the people the number of his victims has quadrupled.

"So great is the excitement that sober minded men who do not see any peculiar interest in the sayings and doings of a great criminal are disgusted that the popular taste should run that way. Be that as it may, the case of Rex v. Sweeney Todd will certainly be one of the trials of the age."

Piecing together the notorious barber's earlier history, Haining found that Sweeney Todd was born on October 26th, 1756, in Brick Lane, Stepney. When he was 12 his parents disappeared, apparently abandoning him, and he became a cutler's apprentice in Holborn.

At 14 he was convicted of petty theft and sentenced to five years in Newgate Prison, where he became soap-boy to a barber who was continuing to ply his trade behind bars while serving a sentence for swindling.

Released in 1775, Todd had learned enough to become a barber himself and by the early 1780s he was in business at Hyde Park Corner. Haining records that the Annual Register subsequently reported that on December 1st, 1784, "a most remarkable murder was perpetrated by a journeyman barber that lived near Hyde Park Corner, who had been jealous of his wife but could in no way bring this home to her.

"A young gentleman by chance coming into the barber's shop to be shaved and dressed, and being in liquor, mentioned having seen a fine girl in Hamilton Street from whom he had had certain favours the night before, and at the same time he described her person.

"The barber concluded this to be his wife, and in the height of his frenzy cut the young gentleman's throat from ear to ear and absconded."

There is no proof that this was Sweeney Todd, but he was reported to have admitted the murder when he was arrested 17 years later.

He was quoted as saying: "My first one was a young gent at Hyde Park Corner. Slit him from ear to ear, I did."

Todd is believed to have re-emerged and established himself at 186 Fleet Street, next door to St. Dunstan's Church, in 1785, a few months after the Hyde Park Corner murder. On the other side of the church, two streets away in Bell Yard, was Mrs. Margery Lovett's pie shop, which was to feature alarmingly in the barber's subsequent history.

There was "something very sinister about him with his pale face and reddish hair" the *Gentleman's Magazine* recalled in 1853. "At times he was like some hobglobin, his strange, dark eyes agleam with greed and cunning."

According to another, even less flattering account, Todd had "a huge mouth filled with black teeth. His hands were of abnormal size, he had immense feet and wiry hair, sometimes bristling with the combs of his trade. He also squinted and was as ugly a wretch as could be seen in a day's march."

The *Gentleman's Magazine* recorded that "all sorts of unpleasant rumours and surmises began to be whispered regarding him up and down the street. For several seafaring men who had last been known to visit his shop had disappeared as completely as though the earth had opened and swallowed them, but no one could prove that he had anything to do with these disappearances."

Apparently Todd was soon back in the business of cutting throats after the Hyde Park Corner murder. On April 14th, 1785, the *Daily Courant* reported: "A horrid murder has been committed in Fleet Street on the person of a young gentleman from the country while on a visit to relatives in London.

"During the course of a walk through the city he chanced to stop to admire the striking clock of St. Dunstan's Church, and there fell into conversation with a man in the clothing of a barber.

"The two men came to an argument, and all of a sudden the barber took from his clothing a razor and slit the throat of the young man, thereafter disappearing into the alleyway of the Hen and Chicken Court and was seen no more." The Hen and Chicken Court was reportedly next to Todd's barber shop.

At about the same time an apprentice was sent on an errand to collect a large sum of money and was never seen again. He had told a friend that he was going to stop off and have his hair cut at Sweeney Todd's, but no trace of him was found on the premises.

Within weeks of that incident the *Daily Courant* reported that the body of a pawnbroker had been found, his throat cut, in a room over Todd's shop. The inquest verdict was "suicide during temporary insanity."

Next, the body of a petty crook who was a drinking acquaintance of Todd's was found in Fleur de Lis Court. "The throat had been slashed with a razor from one side of the neck to the other," reported the *Daily Courant*.

One would assume that with all these murderous goings-on happening virtually on Sweeney Todd's doorstep the demon barber would by now have been brought in at least for questioning. But no official record exists of an arrest or anything eelse concerning Todd.

Eventually, as the story goes on, the barber came unstuck. This happened when Sir Richard Blunt, a London magistrate associated with the city's Bow Street

Runners, decided to investigate complaints of an offensive smell pervading St. Dunstan's Church. The stench suggested putrefying corpses, but no one had been buried at the church for many years.

A preliminary examination of the vaults revealed nothing, but Blunt then heard gossip about the barber next door whose customers were said to have a habit of disappearing.

A watch was kept on Todd's shop and three customers were reported to have been seen entering but not leaving. After that a second, more thorough, search was made of the maze of passages beneath St. Dunstan's. Vaults were opened and the investigators discovered freshly buried skeletons stripped of their flesh.

Following the smells, and the footprints in the dust, the searchers went from the vicinity of the barber's shop to an underground kitchen. A compass and the distance they had walked told them that they were beneath Bell Yard, where Mrs. Lovett had her pie shop.

Blunt decided to search Todd's premises while the barber was out. As soon as Todd went off on some errand the investigators broke in. They found all manner of clothes, hats, old watches and other valuables in drawers, some of which had names or initials on them. This, they quickly surmised, had all belonged to murder victims.

When Todd came back to his shop he was arrested by the Bow Street Runners and handcuffed. So too was Mrs. Lovett, although the investigators were not yet certain what part she had played in the murders.

They were soon to find out, for Mrs. Lovett told all shortly after her arrival at Newgate Prison. According to the *London Chronicle* she made a statement in which she said that Todd had bought premises at Bell Yard which, via the vaults of St. Dunstan's, he had linked by an underground passage with his shop in Fleet Street "by his own exertions."

"When he had completed all his arrangements he came to me and made his offer...the plan he proposed was that the pie-shop should be opened for the sole purpose of getting rid of the bodies of people whom he might think proper to murder in or under his shop.

"He said that, fearing nothing and believing nothing, he had come to the conclusion that money was the greatest thing to be desired in this world, inasmuch as he found that all people bowed down to it.

"He said that after the murder of anyone he would take the flesh from the bones quickly and convey it to the shelves of the bakehouse in Bell Yard, the pieces to be material for the pies. Minor arrangements he left to me. He murdered many. The business prospered and we both grew rich."

So Mrs. Lovett's customers had unwittingly become cannibals. They were reported to have stormed her premises intent on lynching her when they heard the reason for her arrest.

Sweeney Todd and Mrs. Lovett were charged with murder. *The Examiner* reported: "By the time the police office at Bow Street had opened the following morning, a wild, vague and uncertain rumour had spread itself over London concerning the discoveries that had been made at Sweeney Todd's house in Fleet Street and Mrs. Lovett's in Bell Yard, Temple Bar.

"The affair lost nothing from many-tongued rumour and the popular belief was that Sweeney Todd's house had been found full of dead bodies from the attics to the cellars, while Mrs. Lovett had been actually detected in the very act of scraping some dead men's bones for tit-bits to make a veal pie."

Evidence was being gathered for the couple's trial when, as the story goes, Mrs. Lovett somehow obtained poison and was found dead in her cell. She was a wealthy woman, and was suspected of having bribed one of her guards not to examine some clean clothes which were delivered to her from her home.

One of the garments, it was thought, contained a vial of poison which she had previously hidden in the event that she might be arrested.

With regard to the trial, your author can find no reference to it save the reports by editors of penny-dreadfuls many years later, and these form the basis of the following trial report.

On Blunt's instructions news of her death was kept from Todd, and he was not told about it until he set out for his trial at the Old Bailey. There the barber was charged with the murder of just one of his victims.

This was Francis Thornhill, who arrived in London Docks as a passenger on the ship *The Star* on August 3rd, 1801, on a mission extraordinary.

The attorney general, prosecuting, told the court that Thornhill had been commissioned to deliver a string of oriental pearls worth £16,000 to a young woman in the city, and as soon as his ship berthed he set out on his errand.

What is extraordinary about this story is that a string of pearls worth £16,000 in the first few years of the nineteenth century would be worth nearly £2 million today – and that isn't the sort of jewellery a lone man normally carries in his pocket as he walks through the city streets. And Thornhill could not walk very fast because as we shall see he had a limp.

Even more remarkably, given what he was carrying, on the way he dropped in at Sweeney Todd's for a shave, and that was the last that was ever seen of him.

The owner of the string of pearls sounded the alarm and inquiries revealed that they had been pawned in Hammersmith by Todd for £1,000. The pawnbroker, however, had since died.

At about the same time, the prosecutor continued, the authorities were investigating an appalling smell which had been emanating from St. Dunstan's Church for some years. They discovered that ancient coffins in the vaults contained fresh human remains, and they also discovered an underground passage linking Todd's shop with Mrs. Lovett's cellar in Bell Yard.

It was the case for the Crown that the human remains were flesh from the victims murdered by the barber and that the method of disposing of them was to process the flesh into meat pies sold from Mrs. Lovett's shop.

The investigators found that Todd had two chairs in his barber's shop, but only one of them was visible at any one time. Both chairs were firmly screwed on to each side of a trapdoor which, when released, revolved on a central pivot. When a lever was pulled a connecting rod withdrew the trapdoor's bolt. Then the weight of the customer leaning back in the occupied chair caused it to tip backwards with the trapdoor, precipitating him into the cellar as the door turned through 45 degrees.

This revolution brought the opposing chair into its duplicate's former position – so anyone entering the shop seconds later would see an empty chair awaiting him.

The victim, stunned if not killed by his fall into the 15 ft. deep cellar, promptly had his throat cut by Sweeney Todd, who at his leisure stripped the body of clothes and valuables. *(True or make-believe? It would seem that if such a murderous device ever existed it would have been worth a small fortune. Thousands would have paid to see it on exhibition across the nation. But there is not a single splinter of the chair anywhere.)*

The attorney general told the jury that sufficient clothes for 160 people were found at the barber's premises. Among them was the sleeve of a jacket identified as belonging to Francis Thornhill.

Among the prosecution's witnesses was Colonel William Jeffrey, a friend and fellow-passenger of Thornhill on *The Star*. Colonel Jeffrey told how he searched London in vain for his friend after he disappeared, even questioning Todd. The barber confirmed that he had shaved Thornhill and after the shave Thornhill simply got up and left. Colonel Jeffrey said he next went to Sir Richard Blunt for help.

Sir Richard, giving evidence, told the court he began to suspect that Todd was murdering his customers in order to rob them after 13 men disappeared in the vicinity of Fleet

Street, 10 of them having said they were going to a barber.

During his investigation he allowed himself to be shaved several times by Sweeney Todd, taking the precaution of always having a colleague with him. When he subsequently searched the premises he went into the cellar and saw a chair fixed to the ceiling by its legs. It was identical with the one he had occupied in the shop.

Sir Richard described how he had found the remains of recently-dead victims in the vaults of St. Dunstan's and how his inquiries had established that no butcher supplied Mrs. Lovett. Her pies' ingredients were provided by Sweeney Todd.

The court next heard from Dr. Sylvester Steers, who was Francis Thornhill's doctor. He produced a thigh bone found with other remains in the church vaults next to the barber's premises. The femur, he said, came from Thornhill, who had broken it in an accident, suffering a peculiar diagonal fracture. The bone was set but was thereafter distorted, which enabled the doctor to recognise it.

Sweeney Todd's defence counsel claimed that much of the prosecution's evidence was irrelevant. Talk of bad smells in a church, secret passages and meat pies had nothing to do with the charge that Todd murdered Francis Thornhill, who was only assumed to be dead because no one saw him leave the barber's shop.

The lawyer argued that many people could have seen Thornhill depart, and doubtless did so, but they didn't know who he was. Seafarers were notoriously difficult to trace, and he could be anywhere.

Reviewing the doctor's testimony about the tell-tale bone, the defence counsel asked the jury what they would think if a man produced a brick and swore that it came from a certain house.

The revolving chairs took some explaining. The lawyer said that his client was unaware of the trap-door arrangement, which was already installed when he took over the premises. But Todd was later reported to have claimed that he invented the apparatus in order to keep his workplace tidy – to clear the floor of hair clippings he simply pulled the trap-door's lever.

It was "unfortunate" that Mrs. Lovett was dead and could not come forward to clear the defendant, who was a regular worshipper at St. Dunstan's and who was now accused of a murder committed by someone as yet undiscovered.

In his summing-up, however, the judge told the jury they had to focus on just three points: Francis Thornhill was known to have gone to Sweeney Todd's premises; he had not been seen since; and a bone sworn to be his was found in such proximity to the shop as to suggest that the barber had placed it there.

The jury took less than five minutes to decide that Sweeney Todd was guilty. Sentencing him to death, the judge told him that the evidence indicated that Thornhill was not his only victim – there had been many others, spanning a period of many years.

The jury were not told of Mrs. Lovett's confession, which named the barber as her accomplice. The judge now made this known, saying that if she were still alive she would not have come forward to prove Sweeney Todd's innocence. Her testimony would have damned him.

Reportedly, on Monday, January 25th, 1802, the 46-year-old "Demon Barber of Fleet Street" was hanged on a scaffold erected outside Newgate Prison. In common with other criminals executed at that time, his body was dissected. So Sweeney Todd ended up just like his victims – except that he wasn't eaten in a pie.

But did the trial and execution ever take place? We say no, but if readers have evidence to prove Sweeney Todd was flesh and blood and not a character dreamed up by Fleet Street ediors, let True Crime magazine know. *Write to True Crime, PO Box 735, London, SE26 5NQ*

10

MARQUIS DE SADE

Sadistic pleasure and sexual perversion

The Marquis de Sade wrote in his will: "When I die I flatter myself that my memory will be wiped from the minds of men." If ever there were a death wish that was unfilled, this must be it.

Nearly two hundred years later just about everyone has heard of the 18th century Marquis, whose name is remembered as a monster of depravity perpetuated in the word "sadism." Many also assume that he not only invented but also practised all the sexual aberrations he described in his book *The 120 Days of Sodom.*

De Sade was certainly an accomplished pornographer, but he was probably nothing like the monster who lives on in our imagination in defiance of his own last will and testament. In decadent 18th-century France his behaviour was no worse than that of many other aristocrats. The difference was that most of them were discreet, whereas de Sade made little or no attempt to conceal his perversions. He even seemed to glory in them, and in so doing became the victim of his own legend.

Nor was he anything but monstrous in appearance. From police records we know that he was only five-foot-two, fat, with fair hair, a tiny mouth and pale blue eyes.

He did not, as reputed, crawl around a brothel with a peacock's feather stuffed up his backside. Nor did he – as has also been claimed – punish a prostitute for giving him a sexually transmitted disease by inserting bellows in her vagina and inflating her until she expired. But he was jailed for various other offences against women – and after feeding aphrodisiac "sweets" to several prostitutes he and his valet were sentenced to death for poisoning and sodomy.

These goings-on steadily ruined de Sade's career and more than a third of his life was spent behind bars. He was jailed by Louis XV, imprisoned again by Louis XVI, and incarcerated a third time by Napoleon. He became riddled with pox, his damp cell gave him rheumatism and he lost the sight of one eye. None of these misfortunes stopped him writing, which he began to do in earnest while confined in the Bastille.

Comparing his career to that of the Chief of the Paris Police, he wrote: "I may have smacked a few bottoms, but he has brought a millions souls under threat of death by hunger."

Appropriately, he wrote the 250,000 words of *The 120 Days of Sodom* on what looked like a toilet roll, 130 yards long and five inches wide, the separate sheets all gummed together end-to-end. The work was considered so unspeakable that it did not appear in print until 1904, nearly a century after his death in a madhouse. By that time the legend of the Marquis de Sade was well established and his name had become synonymous with sexual perversion, torture, masochism and general depravity.

Although *The 120 Days of Sodom* was banned for more than a century, it is now considered by scholars to be a pioneering, classic study of sexual psychopathology. It tells the story of four Frenchmen, a bishop, a banker, a duke and a judge, who plan a four-month orgy during which they try to experience every sexual perversion they can think of. In preparation they spend a year abducting young virgins, choirboys and others for their experiment, taking them to a castle in Switzerland, where they then indulge in 600 debauches in which are featured coprophilia and necrophilia, together with torture and murder. Described as an exercise in imagining the unimaginable, the book promotes the author's belief that sex rules the mind of man, and that there is no sex without cruelty.

He did not expect all 600 of the debauches he described

to appeal to every reader. "It is up to you to take what you please and to put the rest aside," he wrote in his preface. "Another reader will do the same, and little by little everyone will find himself satisfied."

The philosopher de Sade argued that evil was the axis of the universe. Animals raped and murdered in order to survive, so why should anyone believe that man was any different? God created us to be evil – "he only takes joy in evil; evil is his essence; everything which we do which is bad is indispensable to his plans... God is most vindictive, he is wicked and unjust ... it was in evil that he created the world, and it is in evil that he keeps it in existence – he perpetuates it for evil's sake."

In *The Misfortunes of Virtue* he argued that good people gathered only thorns, while bad people gathered roses, so was it not better to "abandon oneself to the torrent rather than resist it?" In our world the sum of evil was equal to the sum of good, so it was essential to maintain the equilibrium by having as many bad people as good people, and that being so it was better to be bad because the bad ones always came off best.

De Sade has had his disciples – none of whom have explained where mankind would be if his credo was universal. Not surprisingly they included the Moors murderers Ian Brady and Myra Hindley – they had a copy of his novel *Justine*.

It was not just his outrageous sexual shenanigans and his pornographic novels that kept the Marquis behind bars for so long. He was also an influential and perceptive critic of politics and society, and those in positions of authority who kept him in prison for so long did so as much as anything because they feared what he might write about them when he was freed.

Incarceration for the Marquis varied between prison and the madhouse. But according to the director of the asylum where de Sade died at 74, he was not a madman – he was just plain bad, and the director tried in vain to have him sent back to an ordinary prison. The asylum's medical superintendent, however, described him as suffering from "libertine dementia," and reported: "His only madness is that of vice." As that report was being written the Marquis, then 74, was having an affair in the asylum with a 17-year-old girl, his wife having long since refused to have him back. The affair was to be his last – he died a few months later.

The Marquis de Sade was born in Paris in 1740, the son of a count. At the age of four he was shunted off to live with a priestly uncle, the Abbé François de Sade. The Abbé overtly kept two mistresses – a mother and her daughter – in his chateau, where the young de Sade passed his schooldays, the next six formative years of his life, in an atmosphere of sexual indulgence. He spent his school holidays at the home of one of his father's former mistresses, who, together with her mother and her daughter, further extended the boy's sexual education.

As a young man de Sade joined the army and as befitted his aristocratic station in life became a cavalry officer. He soon became better known for his interest in whoring than for his adherence to military discipline. He caught the pox and married an unattractive but wealthy girl, the eldest daughter of the immensely rich Président de Montreuil, a lawyer who had acquired vast acres of land, and his pushy, social-climbing wife.

The wedding in 1763 was a grand affair, graced by the presence of the King, Louis XV, but it was also unfortunate for all concerned. The marriage, a familiar 18th century one between impecunious aristocracy and untitled money, was an arranged one – de Sade being forced to wed by his impoverished family's desperate need for cash. The de Montreuils paid for the wedding and the couple's house, and provided a substantial dowry. The de Sades contributed just two dozen artichokes. But the de Montreuils were satisfied with the bargain, for de Sade had royal blood, his mother being related to the Bourbons, and there weren't many bridegrooms in France who could bring the King along as a wedding guest.

But in that same year of the wedding that same King had the young de Sade jailed for five months and banished from Paris for a year on a charge of blasphemous obscenity. The court heard that the young Marquis had compelled a pregnant prostitute to masturbate with a crucifix.

In 1769 de Sade was approached by a woman beggar, Rose Keller, 36. He struck up a conversation and invited her to become his housekeeper at his private apartments. There, she afterwards complained, he stripped and bound her, flogged her with whips and rods, cut her buttocks with a knife and poured hot sealing-wax into her wounds. When she managed to escape de Sade sent his valet after her, waving a purse full of money. But Rose went to the police and the Marquis was arrested.

In court he claimed that Rose Keller was a prostitute who had solicited him. He told her what he wanted, and she had agreed, going home with him and undressing voluntarily. He admitted flogging her with a light whip which happened to have knotted cords, but he denied tying her up, slashing her or using sealing-wax. A doctor who examined her found no trace of rope marks, cuts or sealing-wax, but it was clear that his evidence wasn't going to be enough to set the Marquis free.

De Sade's wealthy mother-in-law then stepped into the breach. Aware that this was one of the perils when money married into the aristocracy, she sealed Rose Keller's lips with something more effective than sealing-wax – a large sum of money. Rose withdrew her complaint, declaring it was all a mistake and had never happened, and the case was thrown out.

But all this had taken six months, during which de Sade was held in prison, where he was obliged to sweep out his own cell. This evidently weighed on his mind, for he wrote to the jail governor: "Doubtless my parents are to blame for not including this skill in my education. Perhaps you could arrange for someone to give me demonstrations, say once a week for the next five years."

From jail de Sade wrote to his wife asking for certain

curious items to be sent in. One was for a bottle six inches in circumference. His wife complained that she had been quite unable to buy anything like he described and when, she consulted manufacturers of glass and ebony about it they laughed in her face.

"I really do not understand how you will be able to put such an object in your pocket," she wrote to him.

De Sade wrote in the margin of her letter: "That's not where I am intending to put it." In fact, he had conceived the object as a sex toy, presumably for masturbation, for he kept a careful record of how often he masturbated.

Four years after his release from prison he was in trouble again over the affair of the poisoned sweets. He was then living in Marseilles, and on Saturday morning, June 27th, 1772, he woke early, excited at the prospect of another day of unremitting sex. His valet had fixed a morning orgy for him with four prostitutes, and another for the evening with yet another prostitute, named Marguerite la Coste.

De Sade began the day by receiving 800 strokes with a birch. He noted that one of the whores became upset when he buggered one of her colleagues while being buggered himself by his valet. The girls willingly ate the aniseed sweets he gave them laced with Spanish fly. At the evening session he gave more of the sweets to Marguerite, who ate the lot. They made her so sick that she called the police, fearing she had been poisoned.

Sensing trouble looming again, de Sade quickly set off for Italy, taking with him his new sex companion, his wife's unmarried younger sister. He and his valet were tried in their absence and sentenced to death for poisoning and sodomy, despite the fact that Marguerite la Coste and the other four girls had all recovered and had withdrawn their charges. When the story became public de Sade was burned in effigy and his property was confiscated.

Finally the patience of his long-suffering mother-in-law snapped, and she became his implacable enemy. When he moved to an enclave of France controlled by Sardinia she had him arrested and imprisoned. The Marquis tied his bedsheets together to make a rope and escaped through the window. He was quickly recaptured and brought back for trial. Because the prostitutes were now no longer willing to testify he was acquitted of the charges of poisoning and sodomy, but banned from Marseilles for three years.

Undeterred, his mother-in-law petitioned King Louis XV for a royal warrant entitling her to have de Sade kept in jail indefinitely without trial. It is not recorded what the King now thought of the man at whose wedding he was a guest several years previously, but he granted the warrant and, arrested in 1778, de Sade spent the next 12 years in prisons and in an asylum.

He would probably have remained behind bars for the rest of his life had it not been for the onset of the French Revolution. The old King had died and now his successor, Louis XVI, was under arrest. De Sade, meanwhile, was freed by a Revolutionary Tribunal on the basis that anyone who had been imprisoned by the King must perforce be a friend of the Republic. The revolution was then, in 1790, just a year old, and although worse was to come, the horrors de Sade had created in his books were already being upstaged by actual events. The homicidal rampage sweeping Paris included such incidents as Queen Marie Antoinette's allegedly lesbian partner being butchered by an executioner who afterwards wore her vulva as a moustache.

During his 12 years incarceration the Marquis wrote a novel, *Juliette*, which was not published until 1801, when the Revolution was over and Napoleon had taken over the reins of power. The book caused an outcry and its author was promptly put back in prison for his "immoral and revolutionary work."

Almost two centuries later, in 1991, *Juliette* made its first paperback appearance in Britain. Anthony Burgess, author of *The Clockwork Orange*, commented: "Frankly, I can't imagine anyone wading through 1,200 pages of abstruse philosophy interspersed with very generalised scenes of sexual abuse as a prelude to atrocities committed against men, women, boys, sheep or Rottweilers. There's a good deal more incitement to erotic violence in the *Sun*, which is a good family paper."

The criticism summed up de Sade's style – comments about his view of life broken up with sexual anecdotes turning to violence, the whole becoming so predictable as to be overwhelmingly boring. The novel follows the career of a girl named Juliette who at 13 is seduced by a nun. She is the symbol of Vice and subsequently devotes much of her life to enjoying ritualistic sex in which rapes split children open, babies are dismembered, boys are castrated, pregnant women are disembowelled and parents are forced to eat their offspring. In one paragraph de Sade manages to describe a young girl being gang-raped and then sliced into small pieces, while another girl is raped, beaten and has her brain pulped.

The companion volume, *Justine*, chronicles the contrasting career of Juliette's sister, who is the symbol of Virtue and who spends her life participating in ritualistic sex and hating every minute of it. She dies an appalling death, whereas Juliette, or Vice, relishes every minute of her long life. The message is that Juliette has made the best of a wicked world and flourished on Vice, while virtuous Justine, unable to come to terms with it, has had a miserable existence.

De Sade's reputation today, largely derived from such books, is that of a bloodthirsty, perverted torturer who would stop at nothing. Curiously, though, he had a soft side to his character. This became apparent in 1791 when as a maverick aristocrat who had supported the French Revolution he was appointed as a judge to sit on tribunals deciding the fate of his fellow noblemen. In this new role he could have sent all his in-laws to the guillotine – he certainly owed his wife's mother no favours. Instead he spared the de Montreuils and many others like them. In fact he spoke out and wrote so strongly against the worst excesses of the Reign of Terror that he incurred the wrath of the republican authorities. He was briefly re-imprisoned for it, and came close to being a candidate for the guillotine himself before he was released.

When Napoleon later put him back behind bars de Sade continued to be a thorn in the authorities' side. His trenchant pen was still much feared, and in 1803 he was conveniently declared insane and sent to the asylum where he died 11 years later. In his will he asked for his grave to be sown with acorns so that its traces "would disappear from the face of the earth." The wish was ignored – he was given a Christian burial, complete with headstone. And we remember him not so much for what he did as for the myths surrounding him.

Full sexual satisfaction seemed always to elude him, and in *The 120 Days of Sodom* the incident of the nobleman who is presiding over an orgy is perhaps a self-portrait. During the orgy 15 girls are tortured simultaneously in 15 different ways. The nobleman watches and waits for orgasm, but it doesn't come easily. It is finally achieved through masturbation – and the sight of two male bottoms.

Monster of fantasiser? The world has witnessed a great deal of what de Sade wrote about since he died. He certainly would not have been jailed today for his writings, if anyone bothered to read them, although he may have had his name put on the Register of Sexual Offenders.

11

T. E. LAWRENCE

Mystery death of a fanatical biker

If you had enough spare cash to buy two Rolls-Royces a few of years ago, a very special motorcycle could have been yours. It is described as "the world's most famous and romantic motorcycle," and it is almost as legendary as its one-time owner.

More than 60 years ago Thomas Edward Lawrence – the fabled Lawrence of Arabia – rode to his death on it. He was said to have crashed trying to avoid two boys on bicycles, and the jury, returning a verdict of accidental death, obeyed the coroner's instructions to ignore other, conflicting evidence.

That evidence suggested that Lawrence's death was not nearly as simple as that. But then, nothing about Lawrence had ever been simple.

His death certificate described him as "Thomas Edward Shaw, aircraftman (retired)." Shaw was the third surname Lawrence had used. Before that he was Ross. Even the name Lawrence was acquired – his father, Sir Thomas Chapman, Bt, had run away with the family's nanny and changed his name to Lawrence.

Because the disgraced baronet and the nanny were never able to get married, Thomas Edward Lawrence and his three brothers were illegitimate – a considerable stigma to bear at the end of the nineteenth century. Despite this difficult start in life Lawrence was a clever student. He went up to Oxford in 1906 and from there through Syria and Palestine to write his degree thesis on Crusader castles.

It was at this time that he fell in love with the Arab world, and set himself to learn Arabic. He never mastered the language, and the legend that he could pass anywhere as an Arab was indeed a legend – the Arabs always enjoyed his very English pronunciation because they knew that he was not seriously pretending to be one of them.

Lawrence was a slim, shortish youth with deep set eyes and a wide mouth, and he was a loner. One of his many aims in life was to attain supreme physical fitness, a task at which he worked so assiduously that it made him a masochist. He went without food for days at a time, cycled until he was near collapse, and in mid-winter set out on long cross-country treks, using a compass and scaling or swimming most obstacles that stood between him and his goal.

Yet another ambition was to become a perfect marksman. He worked at this on the university shooting range for hours until he was a first-class shot with either hand, and a pistol was part of his luggage when he arrived in Beirut in 1909 to research for his degree.

After a 1,000-mile walk across the Middle East, he returned to England to receive a first-class honours degree in history, and was immediately recruited by the British Government to work on a secret assignment. This was at an archaeological dig on a site near the main German construction depot for the final link in a railway that was to connect Baghdad with Berlin. Oil had been discovered in the vicinity, the Germans had obtained a concession, and the archaeological dig, financed by the British Secret Service, was a cover for gathering information about their plans.

Lawrence the loner was an ideal recruit to the business of spying. He established a network of secret agents, obtained the Germans' plans for the route of their railway, and produced maps which were to prove invaluable in 1914 when war was declared. But like many another spy, he had flaws in his character. He developed repressed homosexual yearnings for an Arab donkey boy who he photographed naked and who years later was to die of typhoid in his arms.

At the outbreak of the First World War Lawrence's spymasters sent him to Cairo with the rank of lieutenant. Turkey had entered the war on the side of the Germans, and the young lieutenant persuaded GHQ that he could engineer an Arab revolt against the Turks, who were their masters.

His instructions were to tell the Arabs that they would be rewarded with independence if they helped Britain expel the Germans and the Turks from the Arab world. Lawrence's thrust was rapid – the Arabs, under his leadership captured the Red Sea ports one by one, and inflicted a colossal defeat on the Turks in a desert charge at Wadi-el-Hesa. But, disaffected with the Arabs as soldiers, he turned his attention to leading them on train-wrecking expeditions, at which they proved much more adept. Success followed success, but unknown to Lawrence his mission was a double-cross. Britain had no intention of supporting Arab independence – the plan was to divide the oil-rich territory into protectorates ruled not by the Arabs, but by Britain and her Italian and French allies.

Lawrence's marauding activities prompted the Germans and Turks to put a price on his head. The Turks advertised a huge reward for "El Orens, Wrecker of Engines," and the deceived Arabs were also after him when they discovered they had been cheated. So it is small wonder that when he was killed on his motor-bike some 20 years later, foreign agents were rumoured to be behind his death. Had his enemies finally caught up with him?

The question is not far-fetched, for Lawrence's behaviour was nothing if not bizarre. He had been a war hero, eventually promoted to the rank of lieutenant-colonel, and had then inexplicably changed his name and re-enlisted as an aircraftman in the RAF. Even if, as was claimed, his war service had left him physically and mentally drained by the stress of living in constant danger, and by the privation he had endured in carrying out his missions, his self-imposed reduction to the ranks was probably unique.

He had certainly suffered in his quest for victory. On one occasion, he subsequently revealed, Turkish soldiers captured him, then tortured and raped him. The legacy of that experience was that he came to derive a perverse pleasure from pain, and claimed that he could achieve sexual ecstasy only through being beaten.

Describing, for instance, how a Turkish corporal kicked him, he later wrote in his book *The Seven Pillars of Wisdom* that an injured rib "made each breath stab me sharply. I remember smiling idly at him, for a delicious warmth, probably sexual, was swelling through me..."

After a whipping, he was mounted by another solider, he recorded, who "rode me like a horse. This degraded me to base level," and left him with "fascination and terror and morbid desire, lascivious and vicious, perhaps, but like the striving of a moth towards its flame."

When the war was over Lawrence turned his back on his fame, seeking anonymity, and escape from the limelight which his exploits had brought him. He reputedly turned down an invitation from Ireland's General Michael Collins to command an Irish Free State brigade, preferring to apply to join the RAF in the lowest of ranks, aircraftman, under the assumed name of John Hume Ross.

But Lawrence had made himself a celebrity, and now he could not escape from that. The recruiting officer who interviewed him was Captain W. E. Johns, the author of the "Biggles" books. Johns recognised the would-be recruit and alerted his superiors. But objections to Lawrence's secret enlistment were overruled by the Air Ministry and he was accepted.

Others, though, soon guessed his identity and when Fleet Street newspapers were tipped off the enlistment of Colonel Lawrence as Aircraftman Ross created a good story. Hounded by reporters, Lawrence despaired of a career with the RAF. Six weeks after his enlistment in 1923 life became so impossible that he was discharged.

Whatever it was that was driving this strange and secretive hero would not go away. As soon as he had his discharge papers Lawrence applied to join the Tank Corps at Bovington Camp in Dorset, as T.E. Shaw, a name he acquired legally by deed poll and which he picked up from the dramatist George Bernard Shaw, who had befriended him. Despite hating his new army life, he remained at Bovington for two years as an ordinary storeman. During that time he kept up a stream of correspondence with the military authorities, begging to be allowed to rejoin the RAF and even threatening suicide if his application was refused.

Finally the authorities gave way and T.E. Shaw re-enlisted in the RAF. If he now appeared superficially happy, the inner torment remained. He confided to Bernard Shaw's wife Charlotte: "I long for people to look down on me and despise me, and I'm too shy to take the filthy steps which would publicly shame me and put me into their contempt. I want to dirty myself outwardly, so that my person may properly reflect the distress which it conceals ... and I shrink from dirtying the outside ... I'm too shy to go looking for dirt. I'd be afraid of seeming a novice in it when I found it."

Nevertheless he arranged for a fellow-airman to beat him regularly. In order to conceal the sexual thrill this punishment gave him he told the airman that his thrashing had been ordered by a relative who threatened to expose him as a bastard unless he was frequently beaten. Apparently the airman believed him.

In fact the whole period of his life in the lower ranks was for Lawrence a form of self-abasement. Despite that, cabinet ministers still took his views on defence matters seriously and he remained in touch with people in the highest places.

Lawrence retired from the RAF after 10 years service in February, 1935, and went to live in his cottage at Clouds Hill, two miles from Bovington Camp, to finish a book he was writing about his RAF experiences. Writing did not satisfy him, though. He reflected: "I think in time I will get used to the feeling that nobody wants me to do anything today. For the moment it is a lost sort of life."

The antidote that relieved his frustration was his high-powered motorbike, a Brough Superior, capable of 100 mph – the seventh Brough he had owned. He called each one "George," and said "George the Seventh" was the "silkiest" he had ever ridden. At the Brough factory in Nottingham "George the Eighth" was being built for him, but he was never to ride it.

Lawrence, always a speed addict, had an expensive taste in motorbikes. He paid £170 for "George the Seventh," enough at that time to buy a small house.

Twelve years earlier he wrote to a friend that when he became depressed, "I pull out my motorcycle and hurl it at top speed through these unfit roads for hour after hour. My nerves are jaded and gone near dead, so that nothing less than hours of voluntary danger will prick them into life."

It was as if he had a death wish. A Brough motorcycle in Lawrence's hands, George Bernard Shaw commented, was "like the gift of a loaded gun to a would-be suicide."

In his account of life in the RAF Lawrence described racing a biplane flying overhead: "I dared, on a rise, to slow imperceptibly and glance sideways into the sky. There it was, two hundred yards and more back. Play with the fellow? Why not? I slowed to ninety and signalled with my hand for him to overtake..."

But it was estimated that he could not have been travelling at much more than 20 mph at the time of his death crash. If he had been speeding, George the Seventh would not be on the market today. It would have been a write-off.

The smash that put Lawrence into a coma from which he never recovered occurred at 11.22 on Monday morning, May 13th, 1935, when he was on his way back to Clouds Hill from Bovington. Speculation about what had caused the crash was intensified by the government's prompt ban on the release of information. The military hospital where he was taken was put under guard and Special Branch officers were posted to his bedside, lending credibility to the rumours that he was the victim of foreign agents. If the authorities did not themselves suspect this, why all the top security?

Lawrence died six days later, aged 47, and conflicting accounts of how the crash had happened went noticeably unquestioned at the inquest. Within two hours of the jury's verdict, he was buried. It was as if the authorities wanted to dispose of him as quickly as possible, with the minimum of publicity.

But the evidence given at the inquest simply didn't add up. The only adult witness at the scene of a the crash, an army corporal, said he thought Lawrence was travelling at between 50 and 60 mph. Yet the Brough Superior was found to be in second gear, in which its maximum speed was 39 mph. And the damage to the motorbike indicated that its speed was a lot lower than that.

The compulsory wearing of crash-helmets was not introduced until many years later, and the injuries Lawrence received, unprotected as he was, were severe. His skull was fractured, his brain lacerated. His death certificate recorded that he died from "congestion of the lungs and heart failure arising from these injuries, sustained on being thrown from his motor-cycle when colliding with a pedal-cyclist."

The army corporal testified that he thought Lawrence swerved to avoid a black car which appeared to force him off the road. He then careered out of control and collided with one of two boys who were cycling ahead. But both boys said they had not seen a car, and the one who was injured required no more than a patch of sticking-plaster, which seemed out of keeping with the army corporal's estimate of the motorbike's speed.

In his summing-up, the coroner told the jury that whether a car was involved was irrelevant. Lawrence had either had a motorcycle accident, or he hadn't. The jury dutifully returned the verdict the coroner clearly wanted, and that was that. Or so officialdom hoped.

The security cover-up and the way the inquest was conducted provoked immediate suspicion that there was much more to Lawrence's death than had been disclosed, and conspiracy theorists made the most of it. The black car assumed the importance that a certain white Fiat was to assume many years later in the crash that killed Princess Diana. Who was in the black car? Foreign agents? Many years later it was even claimed that Lawrence didn't die in the crash at all – that his "death" was contrived by the secret service to enable him to assume yet another identity while carrying out important missions in the Middle East as the Second World War became imminent. After more deeds of daring he retired to live quietly in Morocco, dying of old age in Tangiers in 1968.

There were some grounds for all this colourful speculation. On the day of his crash, for instance, Lawrence went to Bovington, where he sent a telegram to his old friend Henry Williamson, the celebrated author of *Tarka the Otter* and a noted fascist. What made him send that telegram?

Williamson himself explained later: "The new age must begin: Europe was ready for peace. Lawrence was a natural leader of that age in England, I dreamed of an Anglo-German friendship, the beginning of the pacification of Europe. Hitler and Lawrence must meet. I wrote thus to him, shortly after he left the RAF. He replied immediately by telegram asking me to come the next day, wet or fine; but while returning from writing the telegram, swiftly on his motorcycle, he saw suddenly before him over the crest of the narrow road across Egdon Heath two boys on bicycles, and braked and turned off lest he hurt them; and the temples of his brain were broken."

Lawrence had been urged by Williamson to seize power while he was still, a national hero. He would no doubt have attracted a great deal of support in Britain, for the British fascist movement, led by Oswald Mosley and his Blackshirts, were holding well-attended rallies. Plenty of people saw fascism as the only answer to burgeoning communism, and reporters besieged Lawrence's home, demanding to know if he were really going to meet Hitler. But Lawrence wouldn't talk, and one of the more persistent newspapermen departed with a black eye. All these events prompted claims that Lawrence was murdered to stop him organising a political coup – why else, the press insisted, was the alleged accident shrouded by a security black-out? According to the *Daily Express,* he had "the plans for the defence of England in his head."

Lawrence may not have wanted to talk to the press, but one report claimed that he had hinted to a neighbour that he had been asked to re-organise the nation's defence. If this seems unlikely over-the-garden-fence chat down in deepest Dorset, it is at any rate a fact that he had been invited to a meeting at which the Prime Minister, Stanley Baldwin, was going to be present.

The most likely explanation of what happened at the scene of the crash is that a combination of circumstances led to Lawrence's death. Although the road was straight it was narrow, with dips which could conceal oncoming vehicles.

The two young cyclists said that when they heard the motorbike behind them they switched from riding two-abreast to single file. But did they do this soon enough, before the motorcycle was upon them? The direction of the wind on that morning would have carried the sound of the vehicle away from them, so they would not have heard it until it was close behind them. And those dips in the road could have hidden them from Lawrence until the last moment.

The accident wasn't actually seen by the army corporal – he saw only the immediate aftermath. He said he saw a black car, but he didn't see it force Lawrence off the road, it was just his theory that that was the way it must have happened. The boys didn't notice the car possibly because they were too shocked by the crash.

Perhaps it was an unpremeditated accident, with the

authorities unfortunately creating their own mystery by over-reacting with a news black-out. Or perhaps it was suicide.

Support for that theory arose in September, 1966, when it was revealed that letters written by Lawrence only days before his death showed that he was feeling deeply depressed. "I imagine that leaves must feel like this," he wrote, "after they have fallen from their tree and until they die."

Those who scoffed at this idea pointed out that it was hardly likely that a man contemplating suicide would invite a celebrity like Henry Williamson to visit him next day, only minutes before the fatal accident. He would not have wantonly endangered the lives of two young cyclists, nor, as a motorbike enthusiast, would he have sacrificed such a valuable and cherished machine. If Lawrence had wanted to commit suicide, it was argued, he would much more likely have taken a gun and shot himself.

He was known anyway to suffer the mood-swings of a manic-depressive – on a high one moment, in the depths of despair the next. His last letters, it was argued, were merely a reflection of this.

After the accident, Lawrence's brother sold "George the Seventh" back to its manufacturers, who repaired it and sold it on. Still bearing the marks of the accident on its front mudguard, it was rediscovered in 1963, unrecognised and ignominiously attached to a sidecar. Its Portsmouth buyer paid only £1 for it, spent £19 on repairs, and entered it in a rally of Brough Superiors. He knew nothing of its history until he received its log book from the vehicle licensing authority and discovered that it was first registered by "T. E. Shaw."

The machine subsequently changed hands again in the 1970s, the Portsmouth owner selling it to a Hampshire enthusiast for a figure in the region of £5,000, the deal also including a Vincent Rapide in part-exchange.

When it was next reported to be on the market again, in 1997, an auctioneer said that £1.5 million had been offered, but as much as £2 million was expected. Fears were expressed that the machine would leave the country because only a wealthy connoisseur living abroad would be able to afford that kind of money.

In fact two years later George the Seventh remained in England and it also remained unsold. An authority on vintage motorcycles said in 1999 that a figure of around £200,000 would be more realistic. The same model in good condition commanded about £50,000, but the value of George the Seventh would be approximately quadrupled by its historic link with Lawrence of Arabia. This would make it coveted not only by motorcycle enthusiasts but also by collectors of Lawrence memorabilia.

The 998 cc Brough Superior SS100, registration number GW 2275, still has the saddle on which Lawrence rode on his last journey, from which he was thrown over the handlebars to his death. If motorcycles could talk, what would it have to say about what really happened on that fateful day in 1935?

12

RASPUTIN

Strange demise of the sinning saint

He was by any standards a weird looking fellow. He called himself a monk, but he was no such thing – rather, he was probably the greatest charlatan of the twentieth century. He was unkempt, sallow-faced, with broad brow, narrow, sunken cheeks, long untrimmed beard and deep-set eyes that bored straight into you. His clothes stank, and beyond any doubt he was, at 30, the most powerful man in Russia.

His real name was Grigory Novikh, but the world knew him as Rasputin, which means "debauched one," and no one was more debauched than "Father Grigory," as he also liked to be known.

If only half the tales told about Rasputin were true, he still remains in a league of his own, eclipsing all over legendary figures of his time. He sprang to prominence just before the First World War, when suddenly all Russia rang with the renown of the wonderful "saint" who could work miracles, and the name of Father Griggor – "Grichka" for short – was being spoken everywhere.

The ignorant millions from the Volga to Vladivostock and from Archangel to the Crimea were told that a new saint had arisen in Holy Russia, one possessed of Divine influence, a man who lived such a clean and blameless life that he was destined as the spiritual guide and protector of Russia.

In fact he was a sex-crazed quack who betrayed Russia to her enemies and brought the mighty House of Romanov to an ignoble and terrible destruction.

As a young, heavy-drinking peasant Grigory Novikh had wandered from monastery to monastery in search of enlightenment. At 28 he came across a new religion, called the Khlysti doctrine, an outlawed sect whose belief was that it was only through sinning that you could achieve true spirituality. That suited Rasputin – he was rather good at sinning.

The cult practised group sex, believing that spirituality could also be attained through sexual exhaustion, and as a born womaniser that suited Rasputin too.

He told his conquests that only by having something to repent could they achieve purification, explaining to them that when he bedded them he was actually doing them a spiritual favour. And such was his personal magnetism that they believed him. They thought they were having sex with a saint.

His wife endured his philandering with resigned stoicism. "Each must bear his cross, and that is his," she told a shocked visitor who walked in on him as he was "saving" yet another follower.

Moving to an apartment in St. Petersburg in 1903, Rasputin soon became a fashionable mystic, attracting a coterie of wealthy women. One of them, the wife of a prosperous merchant, recalled attending his teatime "at home" to listen to his fervent preaching.

He would embrace each follower, "kissing her on the lips," and as they left they would whisper to his maid, "begging for Father Grigory's dirty linen – with his sweat, if possible."

A wealthy widow joined his string of mistresses who devotedly sewed his nail-clippings into their underwear. Convinced of his saintliness, she recorded that he was "busying himself so loathsomely only for my benefit and purification." His devotees had not time for his critics – a grand duchess dismissed her nanny when she complained that Rasputin had raped her.

A well-known publisher was later to describe seeing Rasputin beating off another admirer, Madame Lokhinta. "She was holding on to his member while shouting out 'You are God!'" he recalled.

Rasputin spiralled upwards through Russian high society so rapidly that it was perhaps inevitable that he should meet and then sinisterly entrance the gullible Empress Alexandra. Called to the palace on the basis of his sham reputation as a healer he told her, "O gracious lady, I am but a poor and unlettered wanderer, unfamiliar with palaces. My sphere is the in the houses of the very poor in order to direct, to advise and to succour them. Such is God's will."

Her husband, the Tsar, noted: "He made a remarkably strong impression on Her Majesty and me, and instead of five minutes, our conversation lasted well over an hour."

The Empress was enchanted. Her only son Alexei, the heir to the throne, was often ill with haemophilia and Rasputin took over his "cure." Many years later, when the mad monk was dead, a chemist in Petrograd disclosed that he used to sell to Rasputin a compound which, when used in strong doses, induced dangerous haemorrhaging.

Rasputin would administer this poison to the young prince, after "prophesying" that his condition would worsen, and then he would "prophesy" the boy would be cured simply by stopping the doses. He also used hypnosis to staunch Alexei's bleeding, and this, coupled with the mystic's mesmeric eyes, soon made the Empress his slave.

Another woman who succumbed to him recalled that "someone terrifying and ruthless was gazing at me from the depths of those almost hidden pupils." The Empress, less critical, simply adored him. There is no proof that they had sex, but her correspondence suggests that they did. In a 1914 telegram the Empress cabled Rasputin: "I shall be back in eight days. I sacrifice my husband and my heart to you. Pray and bless. Love and kisses darling."

And in a letter to the mad monk, she wrote: "How

wearisome it is for me without you... I am calm in my soul, but I am able to rest only when you, teacher, are sitting next to me, and I am kissing your hands and resting my head on your blessed shoulders. Oh, how easy it is for me then: to fall asleep, to fall asleep forever on your shoulders, in your embrace ... Come back soon. I wait for you and am in torment without you."

Part of Rasputin's success stemmed from the fact that the Empress and her female entourage, many of whom Rasputin bedded, genuinely believed that the common people of Russia had innate wisdom, with which the aristocracy had lost touch. They did not know that this particular common person was known as "Grichka the fool" in his native village. In the eyes of his high society admirers he was a holy peasant who symbolised the innocence of the unsophisticated in his refusal to conform to the conventional norms of correct behaviour. They believed that behind his lifestyle lay a greater understanding of Truth than they possessed, and through him they yearned to tap it.

The secret police, who kept an eye on him, took a more down-to-earth view. They watched him hire several prostitutes a day and came to their own conclusions. They were unaware that these appointments were not quite what they imagined. Rasputin told a friend: "The saints would undress harlots and look at them and become more refined in their feelings, but would not allow any intimacy." This, according to the subsequent testimony of several prostitutes, was in fact Rasputin's daily practice.

He also kept his most influential devotees enslaved by being sparing with his sexual favours, and the policy paid off. It kept their passion at fever-pitch.

What did Tsar Nicholas II make of all this after that first interview? He is known to have gradually had reservations about Rasputin, but he was a weak character dominated by his wife, in whose eyes Father Grigory could do no wrong. She wore the trousers and her husband danced to her tune. She even told him to run Rasputin's comb through his hair before major decisions at wartime cabinet meetings.

For Russia was at war with Germany, and the war occupied much of the Tsar's time. If he had paid more attention to Rasputin he might have discovered that the mad monk was secretly receiving huge bribes from Germany for passing information about the Russian military machine.

In June, 1916, the Germans were concerned about an heroic breakthrough made by the Russian general Brusiloff on the Pripet. Within two months Brusiloff captured nearly 360,000 German soldiers and 805 guns.

After Rasputin's death, encoded German documents in his home, marked Secret, were discovered. A typical one read:

"It is of the greatest and most immediate importance that the Pripet offensive should at once cease. You will recollect that the offensive was to be turned into a defeat within fourteen days. But this has not been done, and a certain personage [the Kaiser] is greatly dissatisfied.

"The advance must not continue, and we send you further secret instructions herewith enclosed. Lose no time in carrying them out.

"We hope you have not overlooked the instructions contained in FG 2734-22, especially regarding the destruction of the munitions factories at Vologda and Bologoye ..."

The Tsar, away at the front, knew nothing of this, and no one left behind at court dared question the mad monk. In fact he and the Empress conspired to replace government ministers with sycophants willing to go along with the Empress's conviction that her pet "Holy Father" was God's special emissary.

Prime ministers and archbishops were toppled by Rasputin's machinations. He even persuaded the Tsar to delay mobilising Russia's army against Germany. In the process he made countless personal enemies who he knew were out to get him. He did not need to be a mystic to predict – as he did predict – both his own demise and that of the Tsar, whose regime was becoming more and more discredited by Rasputin's presence.

Revolutionaries were clamouring that the country was being run by a weak ruler and a mad monk pulling the puppet strings, and their hatred of Rasputin was shared by jealous aristocrats who had lost their positions at court because of his evil influence.

"Without Rasputin," the Russian Prime Minister Alexander Kerensky was later to say, "there would have been no Lenin." Between them, Alexandra and her "holy fool" as he had come to be known, brought the monarchy into such disrepute that they ensured that Tsar Nicholas II became the last of the ruling Romanovs.

Rasputin was the first to go. He had already survived an assassination attempt in 1914 which removed him temporarily from the scene while he recovered. He was a tough nut to crack, as his eventual assassins were to discover.

Legend has it that they poisoned him with enough potassium cyanide to kill ten men, riddled him with bullets and bludgeoned him about the head. But he still refused to die. They finally finished him off by putting his bound body into the River Neva and drowning him – and even then he nearly got away.

The truth – or what is as near as we are ever likely to get to it – is less spectacular but no less intriguing. In writing a new biography, *Rasputin: The Last Word* (Weidenfeld, £20), the Russian historian Edvard Radzinsky has had an advantage denied to his predecessors. In 1995 a Russian government file "lost' for 78 years was auctioned at Sotheby's. It was bought by the Russian cellist Mstislav Rostropovich, who gave it to his friend Radzinsky, Compiled in March, 1917, as part of an investigation of the Tsar's regime, the file contained reports of the interrogations of numerous people intimately acquainted with Rasputin, who had gone to his sensational death three months earlier.

The file shed new light on the mad monk and his colourful career, and after more research Radzinsky set to work to tell Rasputin's story. The tales of the monk's sexual excesses turned out to be true, but not the popular accounts of his murder. Rasputin was poisoned, shot, trussed up and dumped in the river, but not quite the way that legend has it. Or so Radzinsky claims.

In the new version, Prince Felix Yusopov and two fellow-conspirators, determined to get rid of Rasputin's pernicious influence on the royal family, met in the evening of December 16th, 1916, at the Yusopov Palace in St. Petersburg. They lured Rasputin there at midnight with an invitation from Yusopov's beautiful wife and a promise that several young women in urgent need of salvation would also be present.

Rasputin duly showed up, and was given the glass of wine laced with potassium cyanide. This apparently had no effect on him at all, so he was shot at close range. The conspirators withdrew upstairs to celebrate, but when they returned to the scene to dispose of the body it had disappeared.

Rasputin was found crawling across the snow-covered courtyard, making for the gate. Shot again, in the back and in the head, he was trussed up, driven to the river, and dumped into its freezing waters.

The assassins thought he was dead, but they were wrong. When his body was retrieved three days later, on December 19th, his hands were found to be raised above his head. He must have been struggling to free himself from his bonds even as the freezing waters of the river closed over him, and he had almost succeeded before death finally overcame him.

Describing the events of that evening that led up to the monk's death in the river, Radzinsky suggests that the exaggerated stories of Rasputin's superhuman resistance to the poisoned wine and the bullets were invented by his killers to conceal their bungling.

Why didn't the poison work? Why didn't the pistol shots, fired at close range, end Rasputin's life? Radzinsky suggests that the reason was that Prince Yusopov was bisexual and that he fancied the mad monk, so he diluted the cyanide-laced wine to the point where it was ineffective. Then most of the shots fired at Rasputin actually missed him, and only one minor wound was inflicted. The bullets which finally incapacitated him, Radzinsky believes, were fired by one or other of Yusopov's accomplices.

Who were they? Conflicting accounts emerge from the file. Some versions say that one of them was another aristocrat, Vladimir Purishkevich. Others say that the fatal shots were fired by Grand Duke Dimitry Palovich, who was officially elsewhere. Radzinsky suggests there was a cover-up because if the Tsar were deposed the grand duke, as a Romanov, was a possible successor.

Tsar Nicholas II was forced to abdicate in the 1917 revolution, and on his wife's orders he attended the abdication ceremony wearing a cross Rasputin had given him. If he was still wearing it on July 16th, 1918, it didn't do him much good. On that day Bolsheviks executed him and his entire family, shooting and bayoneting them to death in a cellar.

13

COLONEL BLOOD AND CAPTAIN BLOOD

Who stole the Crown Jewels?

Despite his cloak and cassock, the parson standing in the queue to see the Crown Jewels at the Tower of London cut an odd-looking figure. He was, someone who knew him once said, "a man with a villainous, unmerciful look, a false countenance."

This wasn't altogether surprising, for Colonel Thomas Blood wasn't a parson at all. He was a former soldier of fortune. And he hadn't come to admire the Crown Jewels – he had come to work out a plan how to steal them.

As Blood reached the elegant glass cases housing the royal regalia his wife, who was at his side, suddenly developed a fainting fit. In fact, since everything about Blood on this April day in 1671 was a bit bogus, it should be pointed out that the woman wasn't his wife at all – the real Mrs. Blood was ill and in Lancashire.

As the fake Mrs. Blood swooned, the colonel called out anxiously, and the Keeper of the Crown Jewels, a man named Talbot Edwards, who was 77 years old, hobbled forward.

"Could you bring some smelling salts, please?" Colonel Blood commanded, and Mr. Edwards, somewhat overwhelmed by the well-spoken, peremptory tone, called to Mrs. Edwards to bring smelling salts at once.

Then, out of kindness, Mrs. Edwards invited the lady to

come upstairs, for the Edwardses lived above the Tower's Jewel House.

"You can rest here until you're feeling better, dear," said the Keeper's wife, ordering her pretty young daughter to bring the unfortunate lady tea and cakes.

A few days later Colonel and Mrs. Blood called on the Edwards, bringing a thank-you present of four pairs of white gloves for Mrs. Edwards, and re-stating their gratitude for her kindness. Once more tea and cakes were served. Colonel Blood pursed his lips in satisfaction. Everything was working out according to his plan.

Leaning back in his chair, he told Talbot Edwards: "I have thought of an idea that could make us friends for life. Your daughter looks of marriageable age, and I have a young nephew who has a private income of his own and is at my disposal. If you approve, I'll bring him to meet your daughter, and we will see if we can make it a match."

Delighted, Edwards invited the "parson" to dine with him. Before they sat down to eat Blood said grace with great devotion, concluding with a long-winded prayer for the King, Queen and the royal family. Edwards and his wife were most impressed.

After dinner Edwards showed his visitors around the sumptuous apartment. Blood noticed a pair of pistols in a case hanging on the wall, which, he said rather wistfully, would make an excellent present for a young lord he knew. Would his host be prepared to sell them?

Edwards consented, and that night Blood went home with the pistols. He didn't want them, nor did he know any young lord, but in the plan he was hatching those two pistols could have been used against him, so they had to be removed from the scene of the future action. Now almost everything was in place for the most daring and picturesque robbery yet planned in England.

Thomas Blood was the son of an Irish blacksmith and might well have had a reasonably comfortable life in Ireland working for his father if he had not craved adventure, and there was none of that in rural Ireland.

There was, though, plenty of action in England, where the Civil War between the royalist Cavaliers and the Roundheads led by Oliver Cromwell was raging.

As a young officer he fought on both sides in the English Civil War. He was with the Parliamentarians when King Charles II was restored to the throne after Cromwell's death, and turncoats like Blood were going to have a hard time of it. Blood went into hiding until the dust settled.

Sharing the resentfulness of countless other dispossessed Roundheads, he now conspired with Irish Roundheads to capture an Irish castle as a prelude to an armed uprising in Ireland. But the King's men got wind of the plot and were ready to defeat the onslaught. Blood's brother-in-law was among those captured and executed.

Blood escaped, and disguised as a priest – the same disguise he was to adopt in his attempt to steal the Crown Jewels years later – he made his way back to England and then to Holland, where he became a spy in the service of the Dutch.

Two years later he was back in Ireland, fomenting sedition. Then he backed another loser – fighting for the Covenanters in Scotland, who were opposing Church reform. When they were defeated and virtually wiped out, he became a fugitive again.

England had plenty of problems of her own, without Colonel Blood. There was a war on with Holland, the Great Plague, and, the next year, the Great Fire of London. Blood correctly assumed that with all this going on he would soon be forgotten. He took on a new guise – this time he was "Doctor Ayloffe of Romford."

But in 1670 he decided to kill the Duke of Ormond, to settle an old score. With a gang of accomplices, the colonel dragged the duke from his coach in St. James's Street, London, and hauled him off down Piccadilly, intent on hanging him at Tyburn.

Some of the Duke's friends intervened, however, and there was a fracas outside Devonshire House, during which Blood fired at Ormond but missed. He fled back to

Romford and straightaway began plotting his next deed of daring – stealing the Crown Jewels.

The day fixed for the presentation of Blood's young nephew to Talbot Edwards' niece was May 9th, 1671. The colonel and his conspirator friends arrived at the Tower somewhat earlier than expected – 7 a.m., but, he explained to Mr. Edwards, his nephew was so excited that he could not wait any longer to see his potential bride. One of the three men with him was introduced to Edwards as the nephew.

At Blood's suggestion, while the young man made friends with the ladies, Edwards showed his companions the royal regalia. The keeper led the party into the jewel house, locking the door behind him, in compliance with instructions.

As soon as the key turned in the lock Blood threw a cloak over Edwards's head. "We're going to take the jewels!" Blood shouted. Edwards struggled under the cloak, and to quieten him Blood brought a mallet crashing down on his head, then stabbed him. Thinking the keeper was now dead, the gang ripped the Crown Jewels from their glass cases.

One of the men, named Parrot, took the orb, Blood hid the crown under his cloak, and a third, named Hunt, who was Blood's brother-in-law, prepared to file the sceptre in two, so that he could wrap it up in a bag.

At this critical moment there was a knock at the door of the apartment – Edwards' son, a soldier serving in Flanders under Sir John Talbot had arrived home on leave.

Opening the door one of the men asked him, "Who are you?"

"I live here," replied the young soldier.

The four men looked at each other aghast, and without stopping to argue, grabbed their booty and fled through the door. As they ran Talbot Edwards raised himself from the floor crying "Murder!" The first person to hear him was his daughter, who had been waiting in an upstairs room for a summons to meet her fiancé.

The keeper's son and daughter rushed out into the street crying "Treason! The crown is stolen!" The cry was quickly taken up and a crowd began to give chase.

Seeing the four fugitives the duty yeoman at the Bayard Tower raised his halbert to challenge them. Blood instantly drew his pistol and shot him. As the yeoman collapsedf, wounded, the four men ran across the drawbridge where the sentry made no attempt to stop them.

The robbers' escape would probably have been assured, but they took a wrong turning. This brought them within full view of sentries on the outer wall of the Tower, who in their confusion began chasing and attacking the pursuers. Captain Beckman, leading the pursuit, began to gain on Blood, reaching him just as he was mounting his horse.

Blood aimed at the captain's head, but his pistol misfired. Beckman grabbed him, wrestled him to the ground and overpowered him.

As the crown was wrested from him Blood said philosophically, "It was a gallant attempt, however unsuccessful – after all, it was for a crown."

Parrot was captured soon afterwards, but Hunt and two other members of the gang reached their horses and rode off. All of them were caught and locked up with Blood in the Tower's dungeons.

News of the raid on the Jewel House became the talk of the town, and windows overlooking the execution site were offered for rent at an exorbitant price in anticipation of a grand day's hanging. Within days Blood's audacity had turned him into a folk-hero.

One rumour had it that the King himself had bet that no man would dare to steal his crown, and Blood had simply taken him up on it. Another story claimed that the King had commissioned the colonel to steal the jewels so that he could squander the proceeds of their sale abroad. Still another story held that the Duke of Buckingham was the mastermind behind the raid because he wanted to seize the throne.

Blood wasn't saying anything. "I'll answer to no one but

the King himself," he told Sir Gilbert Talbot, the Jewel House's custodian.

When this reached the King's ears, Blood's bravado appealed to him. Charles had a soft spot for audacity and he gave orders for the colonel to be brought before him. This it was assumed was merely a prelude to the gallows, although some courtiers maintained that the King would not want to see Blood unless he intended to pardon him.

Blood was brought to Whitehall Palace, where the King sat in judgement with Prince Rupert, the Duke of York, and others. Far from penitent, the colonel said he wasn't too disappointed by his raid's failure. He had assumed the crown was worth £100,000, although he had since heard that the whole regalia was valued at only a beggarly £6,000.

The King chuckled.

From under his cloak Blood produced a booklet he claimed to have written, called "My Sixty Signal Escapes from Imminent Dangers," describing his various daring exploits. And Prince Rupert, the King's general, now spoke up for him, recalling him as "a very stout, bold fellow in the royal service." The fact that Blood had later joined the Roundheads seemed to have been forgotten.

Nothing could stop Blood when he was in full flow. He launched into a fictitious description of a plot in which, he claimed, he was commissioned to kill the King as he bathed in the river at Battersea. "But such was the awful majesty of your unclothed form," he told Charles, "that my weapon fell clattering from my hand. I could not shoot."

Whether he believed that nonsense or not, the King seemed beguiled by the Irishman's effrontery. Charles also bore in mind that Blood had once been associated with the Dutch Admiral de Ruyter – that could make him a useful man to have around in a second war now contemplated with Holland.

"What if I should give you your life?" the King asked.

"Then I would endeavour to deserve it," Blood assured him.

Sent back to the Tower, the colonel considered his next move. Six days later he wrote to the King claiming that his raid on the Crown Jewels was commissioned and financed by the Navy's treasurers, Sir Charles Osborne and Sir Thomas Littleton, and their underling James Littleton.

Blood did not explain why he had not come up with this when he was brought before the King, but added: "Know your friends. I am none else but your prisoner, and if life be spared, your dutiful subject whose name is BLOOD, which I hope is not what your Majesty seeks after."

Charles did not believe a word of any of this, but nonetheless he decided to pardon the colonel. First, though, he decided to talk to the Duke of Ormond, whom, he knew, had a score to settle with Colonel Blood. The Duke was gracious about it. "If the King can forgive an attempt upon the Crown," he said, "I can easily pardon an attempt on my life."

Blood not only received his pardon – he was granted a place at Court and land in Ireland giving him an annual income of £500. To the King's courtiers this seemed an odd way to repay the attempted theft of the Crown Jewels. A writer of the time said the King's motive must "forever be a mystery to the world, unless it was to employ his audacity to overawe any man who had not integrity enough to resist the measures of a most profligate court."

Blood bought a house in London's Bowling Alley, and moved into good society. The diarist John Evelyn noted: "I saw Mr. Blood in a fine new periwig. Exceeding pleasant and jocose. He is a tall, rough-boned man with small legs, a pock-freckled face and little hollow, blue eyes."

Talbot Edwards and his son, whose timely arrival at his father's residence had been the means of saving the regalia, were treated neglectfully. All they received were a grant from the Exchequer of £200 to the father and £100 to the son, which they had to settle for half their value because of the difficulty in obtaining payment.

Colonel Blood still couldn't keep out of trouble. In the past he had been associated with the Duke of

Buckingham, but now a row erupted between them. Blood accused the Duke of sexual misconduct, causing a scandal in London. The Duke sued and won £10,000 damages – a staggering sum at that time.

Blood never paid. The verdict triggered a short illness from which he never recovered. Perhaps he had decided that the times had come for him to quit the stage he had long adorned so colourfully. On August 24th, 1680, two weeks after the judgement made against him, he died.

A contemporary ballad summed it up:

At last our famous hero Colonel Blood,
Seeing his projects all will do no good,
And that success was still to him denied,
Fell sick with grief, broke his great heart and died.

The flamboyant colonel was buried in New Chapel Yard, Broadway, Westminster. His life had been so full of surprises and deception that even his death was thought by the public to be faked. To satisfy them, some months later the body was exhumed and examined. Identification was difficult, but at last the thumb of his left hand, which in his lifetime was known to have been twice its proper size, dissolved all doubts.

Colonel Thomas Blood would have approved of his namesake, Captain Blood, with whom he is sometimes confused. They had much in common.

Both were Irish, both travelled from Dublin to Holland, where both had links with Admiral de Ruyter. Captain Blood, though, was a qualified doctor, and after various adventures as a soldier and a sailor of fortune, fighting for both the Dutch and the French, he retired at the age of 32 to Bridewater, Somerset, to resume his medical practice.

There was another essential difference between the two Bloods. While the colonel was flesh and blood the captain was simply a character of fiction. He sprang, cutlass and all, from the vivid imagination of Rafael Sabatini, an Italian-born clerk who worked for a Liverpool firm of cotton brokers.

Sabatini became a best-selling author of historical romances with *The Sea Hawk,* in 1915, and *Scaramouch* in 1921. With *Captain Blood,* a year later, his fame was assured.

His swashbuckling saga of the Spanish Main especially appealed to film-makers. The first Captain Blood movie was shown in 1925. Ten years later the second one, starring Errol Flynn, was made. More films were to follow: *The Fortunes of Captain Blood,* and *Captain Blood, Fugitive,* in the 1950s. *Son of Captain Blood,* starring Errol Flynn's son Sean, was screened in 1962.

In his books Sabatini had his popular hero getting innocently involved in the Duke of Monmouth's abortive uprising against James II. Although condemned to death for tending the wounds of a rebel and giving false information to save another from the hangman, Captain Blood was spared execution.

His sentence was commuted to transportation and he was sent to the West Indies, where he was sold as a slave. He escaped to lead an even more colourful career as a pirate, becoming the hero of countless escapades on the high seas.

Captain Blood became one of the great characters of popular fiction and made his creator a fortune. Sabatini made more out of him than Colonel Blood would have got for the Crown Jewels.

14

AGATHA CHRISTIE

Agony of a domestic tiff

The Mousetrap, the world's longest-running play, passed another milestone in December, 2000, when it had its 20,000th performance in London's West End.

The Agatha Christie whodunit opened at the Ambassadors Theatre in November, 1952, when food was still rationed, Winston Churchill was Prime Minister and television, still in its comparative infancy, shut down at 10.30 p.m. It moved to the St. Martin's Theatre in the 1970s.

The quaint, old-fashioned play has run without interruption since that opening night in 1952, since when it has been seen by more than nine million theatregoers. How much money the show has made is a better guarded secret than who committed the murder.

Theatre buffs and critics who have analysed *The Mousetrap's* stupendous success describe it as "almost indestructible", with another 20 years of life left in it. They point out that people enjoy the play because they enjoy trying to solve the murder.

Trying to solve a mystery was always the focal point of a work by Agatha Christie. She never had nasty deaths. She didn't dwell on how awful the crime was – only on the solving of it.

She worked this formula so successfully throughout her crime novels that she actually put herself into a real-life mystery that no one has yet satisfactorily solved. On December 3rd, 1926, she abandoned her car near a gloomy-looking pond a mile or so from Albury in Surrey, and vanished.

For the next 11 days the nation was riveted by a mystery which seemed every bit as puzzling as anything she had written. What had happened to Agatha Christie?

Near the pond where she left her car was a water-logged chalk-pit. Police drained the pond and the chalk-pit, but Agatha was in neither.

Other writers of crime fiction turned their analytical minds on to the case of the disappearing detective writer. To Edgar Wallace it seemed to be "a typical case of mental reprise on someone who has hurt her." Dorothy L. Sayers commented that a skilled writer of detective fiction would have no problem staging a mystifying disappearance.

Sir Arthur Conan Doyle, creator of Sherlock Holmes and a keen student of spiritualism, got hold of one of Agatha Christie's gloves and handed it to Horace Leaf, a medium. Leaf assured Doyle: "She is not dead, as many people seem to think. She is very much alive." The medium believed that the glove's owner was in a state that was dazed yet purposeful.

At the time she vanished Agatha had already written detective stories which were to become legendary. Now she was on the way to becoming a legend herself.

She was the 35-year-old wife of Colonel Archibald Christie, a First World War airman. They lived at "Styles," Sunningdale, Berkshire, and on the evening of December 3rd Mrs. Christie went upstairs and kissed her little daughter, who was asleep. Then unexpectedly at 9.45 she left home in her Morris Cowley car, leaving a note which said she was going for a drive.

Early the following morning the car was found down a grassy embankment not far from Newlands Corner, near Albury, 14 miles from Sunningdale. Its headlights were on, and its bonnet was buried in some bushes, as if the driver had lost control and slewed off the road. A small case in the car contained Agatha Christie's driving licence and some items of clothing. Her fur coat was also there, but not her handbag.

Had she simply taken off for some reason best known to herself? Was her disappearance a publicity stunt? Was she wandering the countryside in a confused condition? Or did she leave her car to seek assistance, and get waylaid and murdered?

None of these possibilities could be ruled out, but some seemed more probable than others. The investigators learned that Mrs. Christie had been "very depressed."

Her husband said her mother had died, her dog had been hurt in an accident and her elder brother had turned out to be a morphine addict.

That was enough to depress anyone, and the police also suspected that her marriage was less than happy. This could account for her going off suddenly in a huff, but the detectives had to investigate every possibility.

The colonel didn't tell them that his wife had left him a bitter letter about his intention to end their marriage. Her secretary knew of the note, which he burned, afterwards asking her not to mention it to the police.

A witness came forward to say he had seen the Morris Cowley's driver after it was abandoned. She was inadequately dressed for a cold December morning, and there was something strange about her manner.

A massive search for Agatha Christie was launched, involving hundreds of policemen and large numbers of volunteers—many of them armed with autograph books in case they found her.

The story made headlines in every newspaper. If it was a publicity stunt it was certainly working.

Inevitably, Colonel Christie came under suspicion. Some believed he had killed his wife. He was in a dilemma. In those days every marriage was "happy" until it finally came unstuck. He was loth to admit that all was not well matrimonially because that would attract a social stigma.

Anxious to save face, he played the concerned husband, saying he thought Agatha must be suffering from amnesia. To emphasise his wish to have her found, he paid for missing-person posters which the police distributed throughout the area.

It was all very embarrassing, which he probably suspected was what his wife intended it to be. More embarrassment was to come. For both of them.

The police heard from the missing woman's brother-in-law, Campbell Christie. It transpired that she had posted him a letter in London on December 4th, saying she was going to take a few days' rest at a Yorkshire spa.

This seemed odd, as her husband knew nothing about it, and it didn't explain why her car had been left abandoned in Surrey. But it was a lead. Surely the Yorkshire spa town must be Harrogate? Hotels there were checked, but none of their guests was named Christie.

It was at this stage that the police work became less than impressive. Did they really expect a crime-writer on the run to register at a hotel under her own name? Apparently they did, as it seems they left it at that. The missing woman was finally recognised not by the detectives you might have expected to be mingling with hotel guests, but by members of the band at the Harrogate Hydro.

Having seen Agatha Christie's photograph in all the newspapers, they thought she bore a striking resemblance to the woman they had noticed dancing the Charleston.

One of the hotel's chambermaids, Rosie Asher, also suspected that the guest was Mrs. Christie, but she was afraid to speak up in case she was sacked. The band's musicians blew the whistle on the runaway wife, however, and it transpired that Agatha had registered at the hotel as Mrs. Teresa Neele, saying she was from South Africa and was paying her first visit to England.

Meanwhile it was learned that Colonel Christie had a mistress, Nancy Neele. Significantly, her surname coincided with the one his wife assumed in Harrogate.

Agatha read newspaper reports of the hunt for her with

interest. When Colonel Christie was alerted by the police, and went with them to the Harrogate Hydro to identify her, she echoed her husband's face-saving explanation. She claimed she was suffering from amnesia after striking her head when her car crashed.

"For twenty-four hours," she said, "I wandered in a dream and then found myself in Harrogate as a well-contented and perfectly happy woman who believed she had just come from South Africa."

Nobody needed the "little grey cells" of her celebrated detective Hercule Poirot to find this unconvincing. Ironically, he had made his debut six years earlier in her best-seller *The Mysterious Affair at Styles.* Many now found "The Mysterious Affair at Harrogate" to be much less of a mystery.

For Agatha left a trail of clues which Poirot would have instantly seized upon to demolish the amnesia story. For instance, a mechanic who examined the Morris Cowley where it was found said that it wasn't in gear and its brakes were off. There were no skid-marks, and he suspected it was given a push to send it down the embankment.

In other words, Agatha Christie wasn't in it. She had staged her vanishing act carefully, leaving the car's lights switched on to attract early attention, and her driving licence inside to ensure that the police would know straight away whose car the Cowley was.

The most sympathetic interpretation of her disappearance was that her husband's affair had triggered a nervous breakdown, prompting her to run away and assume the surname of the woman who had replaced her in Colonel Christie's affections.

But in his recently-published study, *Agatha Christie and the Missing Eleven Days*, Jared Cade argues that the novelist's disappearance was motivated by jealous spite: she vanished in order to wreck a weekend her husband was to spend at Godalming with his mistress.

Where did Agatha go after abandoning her car? Not straight to Harrogate. In his research Cade discovered that the children of Agatha's sister-in-law were convinced that their mother knew what the missing novelist was up to, and helped her. They believed that Agatha stayed at their mother's Chelsea home before catching her train for Harrogate.

With the wisdom of hindsight, when Agatha Christie was found politicians criticised the police for wasting public money in the hunt for her. There were demands that the Christies should foot the bill. But the police were in a no-win situation. What would the politicians and public have said if the police did nothing and Agatha Christie was found dead?

True, Superintendent Charles Goddard of the Berkshire police believed all along that Agatha would return "when she has worked out her little problem." But he couldn't be sure. His officers had no option but to look for her.

The Christies' marriage ended in divorce soon afterwards, and Miss Neele became the colonel's second wife. This was probably inevitable anyway. What Agatha failed to foresee when she schemed to ruin her husband's weekend was the humiliating publicity her escapade would bring her. It made her famous, but at the cost of disgrace. She was lucky not to be prosecuted for wasting police time.

That is one way of looking at it, but there is another. Agatha Christie's biographer, Janet Morgan, has dismissed Cade's theories as mere speculation, claiming in *The Times* that he did not speak to those who knew Agatha Christie best.

Nor did he see the letter in which Mrs. Christie's companion and secretary "described what happened on the night Agatha left home and, afterwards, the visits to doctors and a psychiatrist. He has not spoken to those who saw her, sick and bewildered, before and after her flight, when she recognised neither her daughter nor her husband."

Janet Morgan challenges Cade's detailed account of the assistance Agatha Christie's sister-in-law gave her, describing it as supposition.

Cade says that after abandoning her car Agatha walked to the local railway station, caught a train to London and went to the home of her sister-in-law, who disapproved of her brother Colonel Christie's behaviour and was not surprised to see her.

Who is right—Jared Cade or Mrs. Christie's biographer? It seems that despite Cade's claims to have solved it, Agatha Christie's disappearance is still with us.

A publisher has recalled that Agatha was remarkably manipulative. At a meeting at his offices she displayed an uncanny knack of swinging others round to her way of thinking and getting her own way, leaving everyone wondering how on earth she had done it.

So when she consulted doctors and a psychiatrist after her disappearance, was this just to convince the authorities that she was ill? And is that why she wasn't prosecuted?

Like her play *The Mousetrap*, this is a story that will run and run.

15

BLIGH OF THE BOUNTY

Just a bit of bad temper?

The best known mutiny in the Royal Navy was virtually a mutiny in a greenhouse. H.M.S. *Bounty* was in effect a floating garden centre, specialising in just one plant. And its crew of 46 included a gardener and a botanist.

The disastrous last voyage of the *Bounty* was planned when the explorer Captain James Cook reported that on his voyage of discovery to the South Seas he had found an island tree whose fruit when roasted was just like bread. This bread-fruit, as he called it, gave the natives all the sustenance they needed without even the trouble of cultivation.

When West Indies planters and merchants heard about Cook's discovery, they wanted to feed their slaves on it. They petitioned the British Government to introduce the bread-fruit tree in the West Indies, and King George III backed the proposal.

With the royal seal of approval on the venture, the Admiralty bought a 250-ton merchant ship, renamed it *Bounty*, and set about converting it to take bread-fruit tree plants from Tahiti to the West Indies.

The main cabin was extended and converted into a horticultural nursery, with two large sky-lights and a false floor perforated with holes to contain garden pots for the plants. Beneath this floor the deck was covered with lead, and pipes were installed to take the water that drained from the plants to tubs below, so that it could be recycled.

Even in the year 1787, when the Royal Navy was renowned for its toughness, the voyage should have been idyllic and should at least have been completed without incident. And so it undoubtedly would have been had it not been for the officer appointed to command the *Bounty*.

Lieutenant William Bligh was a first-class naval officer who had sailed with the great Captain Cook. In his letters to his Admiralty superiors he signed off, "Your most obedient and very humble servant," and contemporary portraits reveal a man who looks kindly and inoffensive.

But Bligh was none of these things. What Herod was to mothercare, the 33-year-old lieutenant was to man-management. Far from being humble, kindly or inoffensive he was a bullying tyrant who treated his officers and men like dirt.

On board the *Bounty* he was to impose his authority through a regime of near-starvation and brutality. He would have a man flogged or clapped in irons on the slightest pretext. The *Bounty's* rations were anything but bountiful. Ships' crews usually grumble about their food, often not without reason. But the officers and men of the *Bounty* had more reason than most.

The ship set out from Spithead on Sunday, December 23rd, 1787, and conditions were grim almost from the start. It was bad enough coping with the appalling gales that buffeted the *Bounty* without having an intolerant despot as the ship's commander.

As the vessel approached the equator Bligh ordered some rotting pumpkins purchased at Tenerife to be issued to the crew instead of their usual food, which was little enough. Informed that his men were reluctant to accept this, Bligh stormed on deck, had the crew assemble before him and ordered the first man on the list of each mess to be called by name.

"I'll see who will dare to refuse the pumpkins, or anything else I order to be served," he raged. "You damned infernal scoundrels, I'll make you eat grass or anything you can catch before I've done with you!"

The pumpkins were then accepted, even by the officers. But Bligh was already unwittingly sowing the seeds of rebellion.

Tension evaporated on October 26th, 1788, however, when the ship reached Tahiti and the natives proved to be friendly and hospitable. The island was a tropical paradise after the long, arduous voyage around Cape Horn. The crew enjoyed themselves ashore, as did Bligh, who took his time collecting the plants that were to be his cargo. Although he had promised his masters this would be done with "the utmost dispatch," the *Bounty* did not set sail for the West Indies until six months later, on April 4th, 1789.

When Bligh's iron discipline was then reimposed it was even more irksome than before, contrasting as it did with the good times his sailors had enjoyed with the South Sea islanders. The crew were increasingly incensed by it, particularly the 24-year-old mate Fletcher Christian, whom Bligh singled out for some of his most caustic criticism.

Christian had sailed with Bligh before. He was a Cumbrian, educated at St. Bees School and Cockermouth Grammar School. His brother was Professor of Law at Cambridge University, and he had land-owning relatives in the Lake District, where his descendants live to this day. He had got on well with Bligh on previous voyages—so well that he had become the lieutenant's protégé, and had been specially picked by him for the *Bounty*. But now Bligh had taken against him, missing no opportunity to pull him up over trifles and chastising him in front of both the crew and the Tahitians—he had told one native chief that the mate was merely his slave.

Christian had a thinner skin than most naval officers, and each rebuke stung. "Sir," he protested, "your abuse is so bad that I cannot do my duty with any pleasure."

But more was to come. When the ship dropped anchor at another island Christian was sent ashore in command of a watering party. Here the natives were menacing, but no shots were fired, as Bligh had ordered his crew to shoot only in defence of their lives. On his return the mate reported that the natives had become so threatening that he had found it difficult to carry on.

"You damned cowardly rascal!" Bligh exploded. "Are you afraid of a few naked savages?"

"The arms are of no effect, sir," Christian replied, "while your orders prohibit their use."

There are conflicting accounts of the incident three days later which is believed to have prompted Fletcher Christian to lead a mutiny. All the accounts agree that he was accused of theft. According to a diary kept by one of the crew, most of the officers had purchased coconuts and yams in Tahiti, each forming his own separate pile between the ship's guns on the deck. When Bligh viewed his pile on the morning of Monday, April 27th, 1789, he thought it had shrunk suspiciously: somebody had been stealing his coconuts. Each officer was ordered to account for how many he had bought.

"I really don't know, sir," Christian replied when it came to his turn, "but I hope you don't think me so mean as to be guilty of stealing yours."

"Yes, you damned hound, I do think so!" Bligh told him. "You must have stolen them from me or you could give a better account of them. You damned rascals, you are all thieves alike and combine with the men to rob me! You'll steal my yams next! I'll flog you and make you jump overboard before we reach Endeavour Straits!" Then he gave orders for the officers' grog to be stopped and for them to have only half a pound of yams the next day.

Christian was later seen in tears. Asked what was the matter, he said he couldn't endure such treatment much longer: he would rather die ten thousand deaths. "I always do my duty as an officer and a man, yet I receive this scandalous usage." He was clearly at the end of his tether, but Bligh was oblivious to that.

Lieutenant Bligh's tempers evaporated as swiftly as they erupted. It seems that he seldom meant what he said. An hour later all was forgotten so far as he was concerned – he even invited Christian to have supper with him that evening.

But Christian had taken the accusation to heart and he excused himself from joining his captain for the meal, pleading illness. The other officers, collectively branded thieves by their commander, had similarly taken offence and they agreed between themselves that they too would not dine with Bligh if he asked them. When one of them then received an invitation and he accepted, he was hissed by the rest.

That night Fletcher Christian decided he could take no more. He asked the ship's carpenter for some nails and began to make a raft. He intended to desert the ship in the hope that he would be picked up by a native canoe, for they were not far from land. Two of the midshipmen and the boatswain gave him part of a roasted pig to sustain him on his lone voyage, and some beads, nails and other items with which he could trade.

But the ship was too busy for him to make his escape: too many officers and men were about, and at 3.30 a.m. he laid down to rest. He had just fallen asleep half an hour later when he was called by a fellow-officer in whom he had confided. It was Christian's turn to take the watch, and seeing his exhausted state his colleague urged him to abandon his getaway plan.

The officer of the previous watch was taking a nap, and finding that the midshipman due to come on duty had not appeared, and that he was alone for the moment, Fletcher Christian suddenly decided to seize the ship and set Bligh adrift. Bligh would be the one to bob away on the waves, with those who chose to join him, leaving Christian and the other disaffected members of the crew to sail the *Bounty* where they wished.

First, Christian approached two of the crew who had been flogged by the commander. They immediately agreed to mutiny and in turn recruited three more disgruntled seamen. Another trio then joined them, and four of the mutineers went to the ship's armourer, asking for the keys to the arms chest on the pretext of wanting to shoot a shark that was alongside.

By now Christian had been joined by nine mutineers, and with one of them he went to Bligh's cabin at sunrise, seized him as he slept, tied his hands with cord and threatened to kill him if he cried out. The lieutenant nevertheless shouted for help, but armed mutineers now guarded the doors of the officers' cabins to stop them coming out.

Bligh was forced on deck in his shirt and made to stand under guard near the mizzen mast. When he asked Christian the meaning of all this, the mate—brandishing a bayonet—told him to hold his tongue, threatening to stab him in the chest. Others were to say later that Fletcher Christian's behaviour ever since Bligh had accused him of thieving was so out of character that he appears to have had a brainstorm. He had been driven to breaking-point, and he had broken. The bullying lieutenant had turned a formerly compliant, dedicated ship's officer into a madman. But the tyrannical commander's own behaviour suggests he was a borderline case himself. There was perhaps not much to choose between them.

Bligh and 18 of the crew who remained loyal to him were forced into the ship's boat, a few pounds of pork, other provisions and four cutlasses were thrown to them, and they were then cast adrift. The rest of the ship's company, including Midshipman Peter Heywood and two others whom Bligh later said were detained against their consent, remained on the *Bounty*–with 1,015 bread-fruit tree plants for company.

The mutiny had erupted so swiftly and unexpectedly, surprising everybody, that it seems to have been a kind of spontaneous combustion. This had been stoked by Bligh's harsh treatment of his crew and the mutineers' happy memories of the good life in Tahiti, to where they now spoke of returning.

Bligh was later to inform the Admiralty: "The secrecy of the mutiny was beyond all conception, so that I cannot discover that any who were with me had the least knowledge of it."

Describing his plight as he stood under guard on the deck in only his shirt, he reported: "When I exerted myself in speaking loud to see if I could rally any with a sense of duty in them I was saluted with, 'Damn his eyes, the bugger!' and 'Blow his brains out!'"

The boat in which the lieutenant and his companions were cast adrift was 23 feet long, rowed by six oars, and Bligh recorded: "We were so deep and lumbered it was believed we could never reach the shore."

By seven o'clock that evening, however, they were lying off the island of Tofoa, "but the shore being steep and rocky we could find no anchorage or landing."

Two days later they found a cove where they were able to land, staying there in search of supplies until May 2nd. The natives were at first hospitable but when they discovered that the castaways had no firearms they attacked them with clubs and stones, killing the ship's quartermaster.

As Bligh and his companions scrambled back into their boat and cast off, the natives pursued them in canoes loaded with stones "which they threw with much force and exactness. Happily, night saved the rest of us."

They now had 20 lbs of pork, 150 lbs of bread, 28 gallons of water, three bottles of wine and five quarts of rum. Their experience on Tofoa convinced them that they could expect the same reception on other islands when the natives saw they were unarmed. Their only hope, Bligh decided, was to make first for New Holland and then Timor, some 3,600 miles away. They agreed each to live on an ounce of bread and a quarter of a pint of water a day and began their epic journey "without a single map of any kind," Bligh recorded, "and nothing but my own recollection and general knowledge of the situation of places to direct us." The ship's clerk, however, had managed to bring along a quadrant and a compass.

Twenty days later they reached New Holland. They

caught oysters and a few clams there and rested. Setting out again on June 4th, they sighted Timor eight days later. Their voyage—described by Bligh as "the most extraordinary that ever happened in the world"—was nearly over.

When they finally staggered ashore at Kupang on June 15th "a more miserable set of beings were never seen," Bligh recorded. Emaciated and covered with sores, some were barely able to stand. The expedition's botanist, a shore-going man unhardened by seafaring life, died shortly afterwards. The rest made a slow recovery, tended by a Kupang doctor.

Meanwhile the *Bounty*, with 25 men on board, dropped anchor off an island where they found the natives immediately hostile, so they sailed back to Tahiti. Sixteen of them wanted to stay there, but Fletcher Christian was against it. Realising that Royal Navy ships would be sent to find them, he knew that Tahiti would be the pursuers' first port of call. He had committed such a terrible act, he told his companions, that he could never settle "where I may be carried home to be a disgrace to my family."

Eight of the mutineers, including a midshipman and the ship's gardener, swore that they would never leave him, and it was decided that those who wished to remain in Tahiti should do so, while Christian and his supporters sailed on elsewhere. The ship's arms and provisions were divided between the two factions, and the *Bounty* set off again, the crew supplemented by six native men and 12 women.

We now need to follow the two parties separately, beginning first with the mutineers who stayed on Tahiti. They were to enjoy a much shorter spell of freedom than those who sailed off on the *Bounty* with Fletcher Christian.

Before he sailed, Christian had advised them that Tahiti would not be a safe refuge from prowling British ships, but the lure of the island proved too strong for them.

They would have done well to listen to their leader. Shortly after landing on Tahiti two of them were murdered. Meanwhile, Bligh had returned to London with his story of the mutiny, and on March 22nd, 1791, the Royal Navy frigate *Pandora* arrived, sent from England to bring back all the mutineers.

Midshipman Peter Heywood saw the ship coming. At 16 too young, shocked and confused to realise what was happening during the mutiny, he had in effect become a mutineer against his will, and he now innocently rowed out to meet the frigate, accompanied by two companions whose involvement in the mutiny had been much the same as his.

But on boarding the *Pandora* all three were clapped in irons by a "reception committee" which included Thomas Hayward, one of Bligh's loyal officers. Hayward led a search party ashore and quickly rounded up the remaining 11 mutineers.

An attempt was made to find Fletcher Christian and his followers, but when it was clear that they were nowhere on the island the *Pandora* began her voyage home. The mutineers' adventures though were still far from over.

On August 28th the frigate struck a reef as she entered the Endeavour Straits off Australia. Twenty-seven of the crew and four of the mutineers were drowned, and more of the prisoners would have perished had their fate been left to the captain. Most of them remained locked up until almost the last minute as the crew strove to pump out the invading sea, helped by three mutineers released for that purpose.

As the ship was about to sink the master-at-arms tossed the irons' keys to the prisoners, and the boatswain helped to release them. But there was no time to free the four who perished still locked in their irons.

Assembling on a sandbank three or four miles away, the survivors continued their voyage in the *Pandora's* four boats, reaching Timor 19 days later. Finally, on June 19th, 1792, the ship's captain arrived at Spithead with his prisoners.

Their six-day court martial began on Wednesday, September 12th, 1792, on board HMS *Duke* in Portsmouth Harbour. Meanwhile Peter Heywood's widowed mother had written to Bligh from her home on the Isle of Man, seeking reassurance. Instead she received a terse reply which said that the baseness of her son—whom Bligh had personally recruited—was beyond all description.

It never occurred to Bligh that he could himself be in any way to blame for what had happened. Vindictive to the end, he took the view that all who were not manifestly for him during the mutiny must have been against him. And in another insensitive letter, this time to Heywood's uncle, he wrote that the boy's ingratitude to him was "of the blackest dye...and it will give me much pleasure to hear that his friends can bear the loss of him without much concern."

Despite evidence that Heywood had been forcibly detained below decks, and thereby prevented from joining Bligh's boat, he was sentenced to death together with five of his companions: James Morrison, Thomas Ellison, Thomas Burkitt, John Millwood and William Muspratt.

The court was also told that four of the defendants, Charles Norman, Joseph Coleman, Thomas McIntosh and Michael Byrne had begged to be allowed to join Bligh's boat, but it hadn't waited for them. Bligh and his men had made off hurriedly, fearing they might be fired on, and anyway their boat was already overloaded, its gunnels only nine inches above the water. The four left behind included the ship's blind fiddler, whom the mutineers had kept to entertain them, and all were now acquitted.

Heywood's sister Nessy wrote in despair to the First Lord of the Admiralty, imploring him to intercede on behalf of her "dear and unhappy brother." She received no reply, but 15 days later Peter Heywood was reprieved and granted a full and free pardon.

Nessy's joy is recorded in a letter she wrote to their mother:

"Great Russell St. – Oct. 29, half-past ten o'clock—the brightest moment of my existence!

"I have seen him, clasped him to my bosom and my felicity is beyond expression! In person Peter is almost now as I could

wish; in mind you know him an angel. I can write no more but to tell you that the two happiest beings at this moment on earth are your most dutiful and affectionate children Peter and Nessy Heywood."

Heywood remained in the Navy, going on to have a distinguished career.

Two of his companions were also reprieved, but the other three, Thomas Ellison, Thomas Burkitt and John Millward, were hanged, on board HMS *Brunswick* in Portsmouth Harbour on Monday, October 29th, 1792.

So that no one should be left in any doubt about what happened to mutineers, the execution was performed before a party of seamen drawn from each ship in the harbour.

Meanwhile, it seemed that Fletcher Christian's party had got clear away. Studying the ship's charts, after leaving Tahiti Christian decided to make for the island of Pitcairn, which was known to be habitable but uninhabited. When they arrived there his crew set fire to the *Bounty* and sank her. This concealed their presence from any passing ship, and it also prevented anyone from leaving the island to betray them.

The mutineers set about building a fort fifty yards square. For a while they lived happily, building homes and cultivating the land. Then the native wife of one of the seamen fell to her death while collecting sea-birds' eggs on a cliff. Her bereaved husband transferred his affections to the wife of one of the natives, and nothing went right after that.

The natives plotted to kill their white companions, but the women betrayed them and two of them were killed by their own countrymen at the mutineers' instigation.

Things went from bad to worse. Resenting being treated like slaves, the natives killed at least half the white men. Two, however, were spared and another two escaped into the island's mountains.

There were later conflicting stories about the fate of Fletcher Christian. One said the natives had killed him, another that he had gone mad shortly after arriving on the island, throwing himself off a cliff to his death. A third account claimed he had somehow made his way back to England: one of his former shipmates said he saw him in Plymouth 10 years after the mutiny.

The native men were now the island's masters, and they quarrelled over the murdered seamen's women. One murdered another, two were killed by two of the seamen and the fourth and last was despatched by one of the native women.

This left the four seamen in charge of the island, with 11 troublesome women to cope with. One of the mutineers, Able Seaman William McKay, a former Glasgow distillery worker, put his old knowledge to use and began to produce alcohol from the island's plants. The result was so potent that he became a hopeless drunk, and in 1798 he fell to his death from a cliff.

A feud began between one of the seamen and his two fellow-settlers, who killed his assailant in self-defence. In 1800 one of the two survivors died from asthma, and that left Able Seaman Alexander Smith as the sole survivor of the men who had landed on the island 10 years earlier. But there were by now children to keep him company, as well as the women. Able Seaman Smith now turned to religion and began bringing up his "family" in accordance with Christian principles.

The presence of the mixed-blood community on Pitcairn remained unknown until 1808, when a passing American ship, the *Topaz*, dropped anchor and the astonished captain found himself talking to an elderly white man surrounded by native women and children.

Smith made no secret of who he was, and the captain duly reported his discovery, but the British Government, its hands full with the Napoleonic wars, did nothing about it until 1814. Then Captain Sir Thomas Staines arrived with his ship the *Briton* along with the *Tagus* to arrest the mutineer.

As the *Briton* dropped anchor it was approached by a

small boat rowed by a 6ft tall native islander, a young man with black hair and blue eyes and the open face of an Englishman, accompanied by a similar, younger man. The older native shouted, "Won't you heave us a rope now?" When the rope was secured the two young men sprang on board the *Briton*.

"Who are you?" Captain Staines asked the elder of the two.

"My name is Thursday October Christian," replied the young man. "I am the son of the late Fletcher Christian and my mother is a Tahitian. I was the first to be born on this island and I am so named because I was born on a Thursday in October."

Captain Staines wrote in his log that young Thursday Christian wore no clothes except a piece of cloth around his loins and a straw hat ornamented with black cock's feathers. Although his body was tanned by the sun, "it wanted that tinge of red peculiar to the natives of the Pacific. He spoke English correctly both in grammar and pronunciation." His companion, named George Young, was the son of one of the *Bounty*'s midshipmen.

Captain Staines asked to be taken to Able Seaman Smith, to carry out his duty of arresting the sole surviving mutineer. Smith had now changed his name to John Adams, and Staines was so impressed by his "exemplary conduct and care of the whole community" that he used his own discretion and decided to let well alone. Adams was left to carry on shepherding his flock, which he continued to do until his death in 1829.

Was Fletcher Christian a victim or a villain? A bit of both, perhaps. Although he may not have been responsible for his actions, his folly led to many deaths. And William Bligh? Although he became the man posterity loves to hate, those who spent 41 days with him in an open boat would all have perished but for his leadership and remarkable seamanship. Why wasn't he called to testify at the mutineers' trial? He'd been sent back to Tahiti for more bread-fruit trees.

Therein lies the supreme irony of the ill-fated *Bounty*. None of the bread-fruit trees survived any of the voyages – it was quickly clear that they would not transplant from their South Sea islands. The government decided to write off the whole experiment, accepting that a ship and most of her crew had died for nothing.

16

MARIA MANNING

The "Bleak House" murderess

Notebook in hand, Charles Dickens sat in an Old Bailey courtroom watching in fascination as the woman in the dock tossed her head scornfully at her accusers. He noted her diction, her mannerisms, her intense disdain for everyone in the court even while she was fighting for her life.

The woman on trial was Maria Manning, a Swiss who had been lady's maid to the Duchess of Sutherland.

Dickens went home and that evening he expanded on an idea to put Maria Manning into the story he was planning called *Bleak House.* He would call her Mademoiselle Hortense and make her French, and just as Maria Manning in the Old Bailey case was a lady's maid, so in *Bleak House* Dickens would make Mademoiselle Hortense maid to his character Lady Dedlock.

When Mademoiselle, suspected of murder, was confronted with Inspector Bucket, Dickens describes her thus: "With that tigerish expansion of the mouth, and her black eyes darting fire ... [she] sat upright on the sofa in a rigid state, with her hands clenched – and her feet too, one might suppose – muttering, 'O, you Bucket, you are a Devil!'"

In *Bleak House* Mademoiselle Hortense, "like a very neat she-wolf imperfectly tamed," was subsequently arrested for shooting a lawyer who was blackmailing Lady Dedlock. The scheming maid then tried to frame her mistress for the murder.

Reading about Hortense in *Bleak House* we can form an exact picture of how the equally scheming murderess Maria Manning behaved. A petite redhead, she was Marie de Roux before she met Frederick George Manning, the man who was to become her husband, while she was still in service to the Duchess of Sutherland.

Manning was glib, personable, and over-fond of brandy and he spun a yarn to the Swiss maid about his prospects. He was unemployed, but he said that on his mother's death he would inherit some property.

He omitted to tell Maria why he was out of a job. He had been a train guard on the Great Western Railway, and got the sack after a number of valuable items mysteriously vanished from his trains.

Maria also had a secret which she wasn't telling for the moment. She already had a lover. He was Patrick O'Connor, a 50-year-old Irishman she met on the Channel ferry while she was accompanying her mistress to Boulogne. O'Connor was a Customs officer. Maria gave him her employer's Stafford House address in London, and on her return from the Continent he called on the lady's maid and arranged to see her on her day off.

They had further meetings and wrote affectionately to each other, but Maria soon began to despair of ever getting the Irishman to the altar. "Of what good is it to continue our correspondence?" she wrote to him. "You never speak of marriage."

It seems that he fancied he could get what he wanted without marrying her, and he began to play a waiting game. His visits ceased, and he stopped writing. Then Frederick Manning appeared on the scene. Maria wanted a husband. She had all but given up on O'Connor, and she decided that Manning would do—she felt confident that she could dominate him, and if she suspected he was a liar, well, so was she.

Perhaps because she believed what she wanted to believe, she neglected to question him about his claimed prospects. Manning was relieved about that, because they didn't exist.

Infatuated with Maria, he drew up a will in which he left her everything, and that did the trick. Maria primly gave him her hand, unaware that his "everything" amounted to nothing.

Both were 28, and they married at the church of St. James, Piccadilly, in May 1847. Then they set off for the White Hart in Taunton, Somerset, where Manning was to be the tenant landlord. But the job didn't work out. He was too idle to make a good landlord, and it wasn't long before "irregularities" prompted the brewery to get rid of him.

Returning to London with his bride, he became the manager of an off-licence in Hackney on a much depleted income.

This didn't suit Maria, who by now was realising that her husband's "prospects" were mythical. But Patrick O'Connor had come back into the picture. He had written to convey his best wishes on her wedding – at the same time gently chiding her for deserting him. The Irishman, Maria now realised, was financially a much better bet than her feckless husband. O'Connor had a secure job, a second income as a money-lender, and had spoken of investments which included £2,000 in French railway shares. And he was still a bachelor with amorous inclinations.

Contact between the two was re-established. Manning was often away from the beer-shop and the accommodation that went with it. During one of his absences Maria decided to move out. She rented a small house in Miniver Place, Bermondsey. She had most of their furniture moved there from Hackney, and took up residence in her new home, knowing that O'Connor would support her.

Returning from his wanderings, Manning soon lost his job at the beer-shop, so he traced his wife and rejoined her after a tearful reconciliation. Maria wasn't too worried. She knew she could handle him, just as she knew that O'Connor would be a frequent caller at Miniver Place.

She was right about that. The paths of the two men in her life frequently crossed as they came to visit Maria, and they apparently got to like each other. Although O'Connor had lodgings of his own at Greenwood Street, Mile End, he spent a lot of time at Maria's place, enjoying her husband's company as well as hers.

To help out with the rent Maria had taken in a lodger, a medical student named Massey, an agreeable young man who also got on well with the two men in her life. One day Manning drunkenly confided to Massey that O'Connor was "worth anything up to twenty thousand pounds" and had made a will in Maria's favour.

On another occasion Manning began to ask the medical student some interesting questions about drugs. He wanted to know about the effects of chloroform and laudanum. Could someone partly stupefied by such drugs be persuaded to sign a cheque for £500, he wondered?

And on yet another occasion he demanded to know from Massey which was the weakest part of the skull, and if the student had ever seen wounds inflicted by an airgun and if so, had they been fatal?

Massey might have been forgiven if at this stage he came to the conclusion that his landlady's husband was planning to do someone some mischief. But aware of Manning's weakness for brandy, he assumed such questions to be alcoholic ramblings.

On July 28th, 1849, the student left for fresh lodgings. Maria told him she needed his room, and he wanted a change of scene anyway.

What happened next showed that whatever dark thoughts were in Frederick Manning's mind, they were equally shared by his wife. Even while she was conducting her affair with O'Connor, she was telling her husband to order a crowbar and a bushel of quicklime, and lest anyone should think that this was his idea and not hers, she paid for the deliveries out of her own money.

On Wednesday, August 18th, 1849, she went on her own to a shop to buy a shovel, then wrote a note to O'Connor inviting him to dine at Miniver Place that evening at 5.30. The Irishman duly turned up, and that was the last that was seen of him alive.

Maria called at his lodgings the next day. She appeared surprised when she was told he had not returned home the previous night, and she was shown into his room on some pretext. Left there alone, she searched O'Connor's trunk, found his French railway share certificates and took them.

Back in Bermondsey she gave some of them to her husband, telling him to go to the bank and sell them. An hour later he came back with £110. Then she handed him another batch, with the same instructions. On this expedition his nerve failed him. He returned with a confused account of why he had been unable to sell them.

At the Customs House O'Connor's absence from work was noted, inquiries were made and the police were notified of his disappearance. Officers called at 3 Miniver Place, where Maria, looking suitably upset, asked them to let her know of any progress they made in their search for her missing Irish friend. They promised that she would be kept informed.

When the policemen left, Maria decided that the time had come for her to move on. She told Frederick that they must sell their furniture, and sent him to see a local dealer. While he was away dutifully on this errand, she must have decided that she could manage on her own better than with her husband, for when he came back she was gone. Neighbours told him she had left in a cab, taking with her as much as she could carry.

Manning decided that he too must leave, so he took a cab to Waterloo station and boarded the boat train for Jersey.

When a couple of days later two police officers, Constables Barnes and Burton, returned to Miniver Place to make some more routine inquiries they found the house locked and deserted. Breaking in, they began to search each room. Dampness around two flagstones in the scullery floor attracted their attention. Testing the cement with his pocket-knife, Constable Barnes found it was still moist. Constable Burton went to a neighbour's house and returned with a crowbar. The two flagstones were lifted, to reveal the naked corpse of Patrick O'Connor, covered with quicklime. There was a bullet hole in his head, which had also been bludgeoned.

A hunt was promptly launched for the Mannings. Two people of that name were listed as passengers on the liner *Victoria*, bound for New York, so a warship was dispatched from Portsmouth to intercept it. After pursuing a Prussian vessel for five miles by mistake, the warship changed course and the *Victoria* was located and boarded. Roused from their sleep shortly after 2 a.m., the passengers named Manning turned out to be two indignant maiden ladies.

The scheming Maria Manning, however, had failed to cover her tracks. The police learned that a Mrs. Smith, speaking with a foreign accent, had deposited some boxes at London Bridge station, giving instructions that they were to be kept until called for. This seemed odd, because the boxes' labels indicated that their owner was en route to Paris.

Opening them, officers found letters from Patrick O'Connor to Mrs. Manning, garments bearing her maiden name Marie de Roux, and clothes later established to be O'Connor's.

Further inquiries revealed that "Mrs. Smith" had taken a cab from London Bridge to Euston, where a woman matching Maria Manning's description had been seen boarding a train for Scotland.

Superintendent Haynes sent a wire to the police in Edinburgh, where it was read by Superintendent Mowhay, who had already received an intriguing message from a local firm of stockbrokers. They had reported that they had been warned by their London office against handling certain French railway share certificates just before the arrival at their offices of a lady calling herself Mrs. Smith, with some French railway shares to sell. She had a foreign accent, and the firm were naturally a little suspicious.

The stockbrokers supplied the address given by Mrs. Smith, and Superintendent Mowhay went to her lodgings. There he found O'Connor's missing share certificates, and arrested Maria Manning, alias Mrs. Smith. Taken to London and charged with O'Connor's murder, she was placed in a cell at Horsemonger Lane gaol while the police stepped up the hunt for her missing husband.

Manning had also changed his name. Now calling himself Jennings, he was in St. Helier, drinking his way through the money he had received from the sale of his furniture. The Bermondsey murder was making headlines in newspapers arriving from England, and obviously confident that no one would know who or where he was, he actually got himself involved in an argument about it at St. Helier's Navy Arms Inn. Bar customers remembered the noisy newcomer who talked about the London murder as if he knew something about it, and as a new face in the town, he began to be talked about. Word reached the police, and Scotland Yard's Detective Sergeant Langley went to Jersey to check on Mr. Jennings.

Accompanied by Jersey's High Constable, Langley went to the suspect's lodgings at Prospect Cottage, St. Laurence, at 10 o'clock one night in August. "Jennings's" door was ajar, and he was asleep in his bed. Waking to find he had been handcuffed, he admitted he was Manning and inquired about his wife. "Is the wretch taken?" he asked.

Then he told the officers: "She shot him. The cloth was laid on the table and she asked him to go downstairs and wash his hands. At the bottom of the stairs she put one hand on his shoulder, and with the other shot him in the back of the head."

The High Constable asked, "What became of the body?"

"She had a grave already dug for him."

When Langley and his prisoner docked at Southampton they were met by Superintendent Haynes. He took a further statement from Manning, who again accused his wife. The prisoner was taken to Horsemonger Lane gaol, where

Maria, asked if she had anything to say to him, replied, "No."

Checking Frederick Manning's background, Superintendent Haynes learned that in a single year a mail train on which he was the guard had been looted of bullion worth £4,000. Another mail-train on the same run was robbed after his dismissal, and he was arrested with two other men. Those men had been convicted and sentenced to 15 years' transportation, but Manning had been released without explanation. Had he informed on his accomplices, the superintendent wondered?

When the trial of Frederick Manning and his wife began at the Old Bailey on Thursday, October 25th, 1849, the couple sat well apart from each other. Mrs Manning's request to be tried by a half-British, half-foreign jury was rejected by the three judges. Manning frequently glanced at Maria, who ignored him. Both pleaded not guilty, accusing the other of murdering O'Connor.

Serjeant Wilkins, defending Manning, claimed: "Mrs. Manning has from the beginning to the end taken as much pains to improve upon and cheat her husband as to cheat anyone else."

Serjeant Ballantine, defending Maria, countered: "As to the efforts to throw the whole blame upon the woman, they originated in an attempt by the male prisoner to shift the blame from his own shoulders to those of the woman he was bound to protect."

At the end of the two-day trial the jury decided there was little to choose between the accused pair, and both were found guilty.

Mr. Justice Cresswell began to sentence Maria Manning to death, telling her: "You have been convicted of the crime of murder." He was about to continue when, beating her fists on the rail of the dock, she protested: "There is no justice and no right for a foreign subject in this country! There is no law for me! When I consider that Mr. O'Connor was more to me than my own husband, that I have known him for seven years and that he has always felt the greatest respect and regard for me, I call upon you to think and consider whether it is likely that I should have murdered him!

"I tell you, my lord, this verdict the jury have returned will rest on their conscience hereafter. I am not treated like a Christian, but like a wild beast of the forest! If I had wished to commit murder, how much more likely it is that I should have murdered that man"—she pointed to her husband—"who has made my life a hell upon earth ever since I have known him, than that I should have murdered Mr. O'Connor, who would have married me the next month after I became a widow!"

As Mr. Justice Cresswell tried to proceed with the sentencing she interrupted him again. Visibly shaken, he eventually managed to pronounce the death sentence. Some sprigs of rue, symbolising repentance and compassion, decorated a ledge in front of Maria in the dock. Grabbing some of them, she tossed them into the well of the court. Then as she was led away she shouted, "Base and shameful England!" Her next move was to write to her former employer, the Duchess of Sutherland, protesting her innocence and asking the duchess to appeal on her behalf to Queen Victoria. The Duchess decided to ignore her plea.

Frederick Manning, also sentenced to death, wrote to no one. On the eve of the couple's execution he told the prison chaplain that after shooting O'Connor his wife had run back upstairs. "Thank God I've made him all right at last!" she exclaimed. "It'll never be found out, as he and I were on such good terms. No one will have the least suspicion."

Manning claimed he had told her, "I'm quite sure you'll be hanged for it." He said she replied, "I think no more of what I've done than if I'd shot a cat on the wall."

Concluding his confession to the chaplain, Manning said that on going to view his wife's handiwork he found that O'Connor was moaning feebly. "I never liked him," Manning went on, "so I battered his head with a ripping chisel."

When the trial was over Charles Dickens, who was in court on both days, joined a crowd estimated at 10,000 to witness the couple's execution outside Horsemonger Lane gaol on Tuesday, November 13th, 1849.

The spectacle moved him to write to *The Times*: "I believe that a sight so inconceivably awful as the wickedness and levity of the immense crowd collected at the execution this morning could be imagined by no man, and be presented in no heathen land under the sun.

"The horrors of the gibbet, and of the crime which brought the wretched murderers to it, faded in my mind before the atrocious bearing, looks and language of the assembled spectators. When I came upon the scene at midnight, the shrillness of the cries and howls that were raised from time to time, denoting that they came from a concourse of boys and girls already assembled in the best places, made my blood run cold.

"As the night went on, screeching and laughing and yelling in strong chorus of parodies of Negro melodies with substitution of 'Mrs. Manning' for 'Susannah' and the like, were added to these. When the day dawned thieves, low prostitutes, ruffians and vagabonds of every kind flocked onto the ground with every variety of offensive and foul behaviour.

"Fightings, faintings, whistlings, imitations of Punch, brutal jokes, tumultuous demonstrations of indecent delight when swooning women were dragged out of the crowd by the police with their dresses disordered, gave a new zest to the general entertainment.

"When the sun rose brightly it gilded thousands upon thousands of upturned faces so inexpressibly odious in their brutal mirth or callousness that a man had cause to feel ashamed of the shape he wore."

Dickens's letter was an impressive condemnation of public executions, but nearly 20 years were to pass before Parliament decided that they should henceforth be conducted within the privacy of prisons.

Mrs. Manning wore a new black satin dress for her execution. She was so reviled that as a result of her choice of the material it was said to have become unfashionable, still being shunned 20 years later – it was claimed that she ruined the market for black satin. But what was the truth of that story? Research carried out in the early 1980s indicated that in reality the market for black satin was unaffected by Maria Manning choosing it for her hanging.

Dickens was clearly troubled by the public execution of the Mannings. After it was over he was haunted by his last sight of the two figures, "the man's, a limp, loose suit of clothes as if the man had gone out of them; the woman's a fine shape, so elaborately corseted and artfully dressed, that it was quite unchanged in its trim appearance as it slowly swung from side to side." Four years later he brought Maria back to life as Hortense, and in that guise she is destined to live on for ever.

17

JACK KEROUAC

Author in a murder mix-up

The word weirdo could have been coined for America's Beat Generation. Its central characters were weird, wonderful and wacky. They aimed to stand the world on its end and they left behind them behavourial legends that have few equals in the story of modern art and literature.

One such hero of the times was the writer Jack Kerouac. Literary reference books present him as a university drop-out who opted out of conventional society and became a merchant seaman and novelist, exploring low-life and Buddhism in his quest for illumination. In this role he became an icon of the Beat Generation.

What the reference books don't tell you is how he came to be driven from jail to get married, a detective standing in as best man, and was then returned to his cell.

Jack Kerouac was behind bars as a material witness to a murder he had failed to report. And the events that led up to that murder were every bit as bizarre as most other episodes in Beat history.

The story began one night in 1943 when his live-in girl friend Edie Parker brought home one of her fellow-students to meet him. The visitor was Lucien Carr, a 19-year-old rebel against all things conventional, who was always up to mischief. A slim but muscular five foot nine, he was fair-haired and good-looking. He was also intelligent, articulate, well-read and fluent in French, and Kerouac warmed to him.

Carr yearned to be a literary genius, but that ambition eluded him. Instead he drew attention to himself by doing bizarre party tricks. One of them was to open a window and urinate into the street. Another was to munch a beer glass, and sill another was to rip the pages from a Bible.

Carr was quickly accepted into Kerouac's circle, which included fellow-writers William Burroughs and Alan Ginsberg. They all liked the young student because they could never tell what he would do next—like the time he was found with his head in an oven, the gas turned on. What was he up to? He told the doctors who revived him that the escapade was "a work of art," and he was put in a mental hospital for a month.

Following a spell at the University of Chicago, Carr became a student at New York's Columbia University, where he could be guaranteed to upstage anything that was going on around him. But it was at Columbia that Carr became afflicted with the greatest problem of his life – his "shadow."

This was David Kammerer, 35, tall, red-haired, heavily built, and homosexual. He had been Lucien Carr's scoutmaster back in St. Louis, Missouri, and became infatuated with him. Ever since then he had followed Carr around with a dogged devotion that was both heroic and pathetic.

Carr's mother considered Kammerer a sinister influence, and did her best to break the relationship, moving from state to state with her son in an effort to evade the ex-scoutmaster's clinging attentions. But whenever the Carrs moved Kammerer moved too. Nothing could shake him off, and nothing could ever come of the attachment—it was a hopeless passion because Lucien was heterosexual.

Nevertheless, the teenager liked Kammerer as an intellectual companion. The older man was a graduate of Washington University, St. Louis, and Lucien enjoyed basking in his admiration. Whenever the youth behaved outrageously Kammerer would smile benignly, murmuring, "Isn't he wonderful?"

Almost everyone agreed; but wonderful at what? At being unpredictable? Ultimately Carr's permanent position in the Beat circle would depend upon his talent as a writer, but as such he was a non-starter—his pen seemed to freeze in his hand, producing nothing but stilted, boring sentences that contrasted disappointingly with his colourful antics.

It was hard to believe that such poor stuff could be produced by the hip youngster who on a whim once got Jack Kerouac to crawl into an empty barrel, and then rolled him down Broadway. But Lucien could more than hold his own in conversation, and David Kammerer, who was perforce nailed on to the circle because of his affection for Lucien, was no conversational slouch either – in fact, William Burroughs preferred his company to that of the teenager, who was bright but callow.

It was clear to all that there was nothing, absolutely nothing, that Kammerer would not do to feed his obsession with Lucien, who always referred to him as "the old man." Trailing in the youth's wake, Kammerer had thrown in job after job just to be near him. When the Carrs moved from Chicago to New York, Kammerer quit his Chicago teaching post and found work as a caretaker, living in a room that went with the job on Morton Street, off New York's Seventh Avenue. As his infatuation intensified he spoke of committing suicide if Lucien did not return his love, and in a drunken outburst he threatened the boy's girl friend, Céline Young.

Then he learned that Lucien was planning to broaden his experience by going to sea with Jack Kerouac, and he became desperate. Kammerer had spent years faithfully trotting after the bewitching boy. Was he now going to lose him?

On the night of Sunday, August 13th, 1944, Kammerer set out to trawl the bars of New York's Greenwich Village in search of Lucien. Around midnight he met Jack Kerouac, who told him where he would find Carr drinking with Alan Ginsberg. Kammerer joined them in

Broadway's West End Bar, and Ginsberg left for home shortly afterwards.

For what happened after that we have to rely on Lucien Carr's account: David Kammerer was no longer around to tell the story.

Carr said that around 3.30 a.m. he and Kammerer wandered into Riverside Park, near the Hudson River. They were sitting on a bank, chatting, when Kammerer suddenly told Lucien that he wanted to rape him. It was not the first time he had expressed this desire, but he now told Carr that he would rather they both died if he couldn't have him.

They had often wrestled before, playfully. But this time Lucien realised that Kammerer meant business—and he was a burly six-foot, weighing more than 13 stone. Carr, three inches shorter and three stone lighter, was no match for him. It was only a matter of time, and not much at that, Carr realised, before Kammerer overpowered him. So in desperation he pulled out his Boy Scout pocket-knife and stabbed his friend twice in the chest.

Kammerer collapsed. Was he dead? He seemed to be, but Carr wasn't sure. Panicking, he rolled the body down the bank to the river's edge. Then he removed Kammerer's shoe-laces, using them to bind his hands and feet together. He also removed Kammerer's shirt, tearing it into strips and tying them round the victim. Next he collected some rocks and stones, stuffing them into the man's pockets to weight him. That done, he rolled the body into the Hudson.

He was later to say that as he hurried away he thought of disappearing immediately, becoming a merchant seaman, like Kerouac. But he decided against this, and at dawn he was knocking on Burroughs's door. As Burroughs opened it Carr handed him the packet of Lucky Strikes he had taken from one of Kammerer's pockets. "Have the last cigarette," he said.

Burroughs got rid of the cigarettes by flushing them down his lavatory. He advised Carr to tell his mother what had happened, get a lawyer, and go to the authorities saying he had acted in self-defence, fending off Kammerer's homosexual assault. The jury would be sympathetic.

Before acting on this advice Carr went to wake up Kerouac, who was asleep in bed with Edie Parker.

"I disposed of the old man," Carr announced.

"What in hell didja go and do that for?" asked Kerouac.

Carr replied that before turning himself in he wanted them to have a last drink together, so they made their way to Harlem via Morningside Park, where Carr buried Kammerer's spectacles. Kerouac said he would act as look-out while Carr disposed of the murder weapon by dropping it down a subway grate. But Carr—forever an exhibitionist—could not bring himself to do this surreptitiously. Instead, in full view of passers-by, he dramatically knelt by the grate and let go of his Scout knife. It was as if, Kerouac later recorded, it "was the one thing he really didn't want to hide."

They went to a bar and ordered cold beers, moved on to a cinema to see *The Four Feathers*, and visited the Museum of Modern Art to view the exhibits. After they parted Carr went to his mother's home on East 57th Street and told her all. She found him a lawyer, who took him to the district attorney.

By now three days had passed since the killing. Kammerer had not been reported missing, no body had turned up in the Hudson, and the authorities suspected that Carr was fantasising.

Detained overnight while the police investigated, he passed the time reading poetry—which included Rimbaud's *A Season in Hell*.

Then he led detectives to the spot where he had buried Kammerer's glasses, which were recovered. The party moved on to Riverside Park, where he re-enacted the struggle. There was still no body, and the detectives took him back to the DA's office.

A few hours later a coastguard reported a corpse floating in the Hudson River off 108th Street. Minutes after it was taken from the water police drove Carr to identify it, and then charged him with second-degree homicide.

Kerouac and Burroughs were picked up and held as material witnesses, and Carr made his first court appearance on August 17th. According to a newspaper report, he "listened lackadaisically" and said nothing as he was ordered to be held without bail pending a hearing on August 29th. His lawyer raised no objection to the accused being sent to hospital for psychiatric observation.

William Burroughs was released from custody, his father providing bail and taking him home to St. Louis. Meanwhile Jack Kerouac, locked up in Bronx County Jail, tried unsuccessfully to raise bail.

Edie Parker's parents offered to come up with the necessary cash if he married her. Neither Kerouac nor Edie had considered marriage seriously, but now it seemed a good idea.

On August 22nd Kerouac was driven to City Hall for the brief ceremony, with Carr's girl friend Céline as the bridesmaid.

The reception was confined to a few drinks at a nearby bar, and then Kerouac was returned to prison to await the promised bail. He had earlier been taken to the morgue to confirm the body's identification, and he was surprised to see that despite being immersed for three days the penis was still erect.

Kerouac was released a few days later, and in October Lucien Carr, pleading guilty to first-degree manslaughter, was sentenced to one to 20 years' imprisonment. After serving two years he was released in 1946.

Ironically, the antics of over-the-top Lucien were eclipsed six years later by Burroughs in a William Tell-style killing. At a party his wife told him to shoot a champagne glass off her head. He took aim...and missed, his bullet passing through her brain.

He forfeited bail and left the country, later learning that he had been given a two-year suspended sentence in his absence. And in true Beat Generation style, his defence lawyer fled to Brazil after shooting to death a youth who had accidentally damaged his car!

18

ETHEL PROUDLOCK

Colonial temptress – or innocent ex-pat?

Ever since Shakespeare wrote *Measure for Measure,* writers have been fascinated by the simple plot idea of a woman who sacrifices everything in defence of her honour. E. M. Forster's *A Passage to India* revolves upon a woman's honour, and so does William Somerset Maugham's celebrated play *The Letter.*

Maugham's play depends on more than that. It depends on an event that really happened.

Maugham was visiting Malaysia in the early 1920s when he was told the story of Mrs. Ethel Mabel Proudlock by a Singapore lawyer named Courtenay Dickinson.

He learned that a decade had passed since Mrs. Proudlock made headlines in what was then the British colony. She was a 23-year-old blonde, mother of a child and the wife of William Proudlock, 33, who was acting headmaster of Kuala Lumpur's Victoria Institution, a school for the sons of colonial officials.

After attending evensong at her local church on Sunday, April 23rd, 1911, Ethel Proudlock turned down a dinner invitation for that night, saying that as her husband would be out on business that evening she wanted to stay home and catch up on her correspondence.

As soon as she arrived home she changed into a sleeveless gown with a plunging neckline. The reason for that, she was later to say, was to keep cool during the stifling hot, rainy evening. Her little daughter Dorothy was asleep in bed, and Ethel settled down to write her letters.

The Proudlocks' bungalow looked out on to the town's High Street, but that evening the view was obscured by heavy rain. Ethel was not expecting any callers, although she had issued a casual invitation to her husband's friend William Crozier Steward, so she wasn't altogether surprised when a rickshaw appeared in the gloom at her gate and deposited Steward, an engineer who managed a local tin-mine.

At the front door she told him: "Will is dining out with one of his teachers tonight." The visitor did not turn and go back down the drive, so she invited him in and offered him a chair. He did not seem to be in a hurry to leave and as he settled down they talked about the weather, the flooded river and church affairs. She got up to fetch him a book about agnosticism, and he followed her.

"He put his right arm round my waist, drew me to him and kissed me," she said. "I asked him if he were not mad. He said, 'Never mind the book. You do look bonny. I love you. Let me have you. I must have you.'

"He put out the light, holding me, and pulled up my dress. He put his hand on my person. I wrenched [his hand] away. He pressed me to him. I stretched my hand to switch on the lights and my hand came into contact with the revolver on the bookcase... I grasped it.... I think I must have fired twice."

In fact she couldn't really be sure how many times she fired it, she said, because she was so frightened that her mind had gone blank. "That is all I remember. I remember stumbling somewhere, but I don't know where. I think it was on the steps, but I'm not sure. I do not know what happened after the first shot."

The rickshaw man was waiting, as Steward had instructed him, under some trees about 20 yards from the verandah. He told the police that he heard two shots, and as he approached the bungalow to see if anything was wrong, the front door opened and Steward staggered out, clutching his chest and stumbling down the steps. The rickshaw man turned and ran back to the street. As he ran he heard three more shots. He looked over his shoulder and saw Mrs. Proudlock holding a gun. She was standing over Steward, who was now sprawled on the ground.

It was later established that the first two shots from the Webley revolver had hit the victim in the chest and neck. Ethel Proudlock said she could not recall firing three more bullets which had ploughed into his head. She was dazed for several minutes, she said, and she then called her houseboy-cum-cook from his room and sent him to fetch her husband.

William Proudlock came running from his dinner appointment a quarter of an hour later. His wife's first words to him were: "Blood! Blood! Oh, Will, I've shot a man!"

"What man? Who is he?" Proudlock replied.

"Mr. Steward... He ran, he ran. ..." She pointed to the body of Steward, lying on the front drive. Proudlock bent over the body, which was still warm, the head lying in a puddle of blood. When the police arrived shortly afterwards they noticed that footprints close to the body matched Ethel Proudlock's shoes, and the gun lay further away on the ground. Ethel was arrested and taken to the police station.

Next day she appeared before magistrates, charged with causing William Steward's death. It was understood that she had fired in self-defence to protect her honour, but no evidence was given, the presiding magistrate saying that he wished to spare her as much embarrassment as possible. Instead of being remanded in custody, as was customary for anyone facing such a serious charge, she was allowed to return home.

Attitudes had changed, however, by the time Ethel Proudlock made her next court appearance seven days later. Her innocence was no longer being taken for granted.

As the depositions were written down it became apparent that the prosecutor did not believe her account of what had happened. There was no medical evidence of rape or attempted rape, he told the court. William Steward's trousers were not unbuttoned, and the only sign of a struggle having taken place was an upset tea-caddy. And although the defendant's husband had confirmed that she wore a low-cut dress even when dining by herself, the prosecutor raised an eyebrow at this, indicating that this was something else he found hard to believe.

Bail was refused when the court rose at the end of the day, and Ethel Proudlock was taken to the local jail. Apart from trips to court, she was to see nowhere else for the next ten weeks.

On the second day of the committal hearing her husband testified that on the day of the shooting he and his wife had gone to sleep during the afternoon. After tea on the verandah they did some target practice with the revolver which his wife had bought him for his birthday five days previously. Then, before they went to church he had given the gun to Ethel, telling her to put it in a safe place. After the service they called at the Selangor Club for a few minutes, and then returned home. He then changed his clothes and went out to dine at the home of a colleague named Ambler.

When he was called home, Mr. Proudlock continued, he found his wife very pale, unintelligible and in tears. There was blood on her face and tea-gown, and she seemed wild and excited. He could see there had been some kind of a struggle, and he saw bruises on Ethel's legs and shoulders the next day.

Replying to counsel's questions, he said he and Ethel were happily married and he had never had any reason to complain about her morals. William Steward had always treated her as a gentleman should, and Mr. Proudlock said he regarded him as a friend. He had known him for nearly two years.

Asked about his wife's parents, her husband said that his wife's father was European but after his marriage he had heard that her mother might be Asian.

The court was told that no bruises had been found on Mrs. Proudlock by a doctor who examined her on the night of the shooting, and the prosecutor suggested the injuries were self-inflicted.

The hearing resumed the next day and Ethel Proudlock broke down in tears when she was committed for trial on a charge of murdering William Steward. Through her defence counsel she indicated that she would plead not guilty.

By the time the trial opened on June 12th, 1911, local gossips had decided that Steward had been her lover. But were they right?

The rickshaw driver testified that he saw the *tuan* (master) run from the house and collapse. He saw the *mem* (mistress) stand near the *tuan.* He heard the *tuan* groan and then he was silent. The *mem* said nothing. He asked her, "*Apa ini, Mem?*" ("What is it, mistress?"), but she did not reply.

The doctor who conducted a post-mortem examination told the court: "One bullet entered the skull above the right ear, a second bullet entered the skull behind the left ear. A third entered the nape of the neck, a fourth entered at the angle of the left jaw and there was a fifth wound an eighth of an inch below the last. The last bullet entered the right breast.

"When the body was found in the drive by the assistant surgeon he observed a wound in the left temple from which brain matter was protruding and blood was oozing."

So from the doctor's evidence it appeared that Steward had been shot six times, not five as was originally supposed.

Giving evidence, Ethel confirmed that, like her husband, she had known William Steward for about two years, and he often dined with the couple at their home. She had seen him at the club the day before the shooting, and she had casually suggested that he should call.

"But mind you come before nine or at any rate soon after," she had told him. "We retire early."

Her account of the shooting was unconvincing. First she said she intended to fire above Steward's head to scare him. Then she said she didn't know the gun was loaded.

The prosecution suggested that her relationship with Steward was rather more intimate than she described. It was claimed that the two had been lovers for about a year, carrying on their affair both at Ethel's home when her husband was away and at Steward's home at Salak South, a few miles from Kuala Lumpur, which Ethel had often visited alone, although sometimes she was accompanied by her infant daughter.

It was alleged that when her husband went to Hong Kong for three weeks, Ethel spent a whole night at Steward's home. On another occasion she gave a small dinner party during her husband's absence. Steward was one of the guests, and he and Ethel spent the greater part of the evening not at the table but in the back of his car. Steward arrived for the dinner party at nine o'clock, and did not leave until two the next morning.

To all these accusations Mrs. Proudlock replied, "Never." And the prosecution was unable to substantiate them.

But a witness testified that William Steward had acquired a Chinese mistress about three months before his murder. When the police went to Steward's home they found a Chinese woman there. Told that he was dead, she wept. So did he drop Ethel for his Chinese mistress, and did Ethel shoot him in revenge?

Why did she buy a gun for her husband only five days before the murder? She told friends that she decided on a revolver as a birthday present because her husband liked nothing better than shooting crocodiles. This surprised some of his acquaintances, who thought his favourite recreation was playing the piano, and shooting crocodiles with a handgun would also be rather futile.

Witnesses were called to support the prosecution's claim that Ethel had been a lot closer to Steward than she was prepared to admit. As they gave evidence Ethel in the dock did her best to look a picture of injured innocence. Her counsel told Mr. Justice Seccombe Smith that she had instructed him to say that she would rather be convicted of murder than leave the court tainted with adultery.

The judge was unimpressed. "You remember certain trivial things," he told Ethel, "but you do not remember other important things. Can you explain how you remember the first shot and no more? Are you honestly telling us that between the first shot and the time of calling the houseboy your mind is unable to tell us anything?"

The defence called medical experts who testified that Ethel was nervous, and disposed to become hysterical. Attempted rape would trigger in such a woman an attack of hysteria that would cause her to lose consciousness.

Mr. Justice Seccombe Smith then decided to put to Edith the sort of questions that women witnesses at the beginning of the twentieth century did not like answering in open court.

'What sort of underwear were you wearing on the night of the shooting?" he asked her.

"Stockings and a chemise," Edith replied.

"Was it your habit to wear underclothes like that?"

"Yes it is, when I am wearing a tea-gown in the evening."

"Were you not wearing knickers?"

"No. I am not in the habit of wearing them when I wear a frock with a thick lining."

The drift of the judge's questions left little doubt about what he was thinking. Ethel and Steward had apparently been seeing less of each other in the weeks preceding the shooting. So did she dress for seduction, hoping to win her lover back from his Chinese mistress? Did she then shoot him when he told her their affair was over?

Or was Ethel desperately defending her honour, as she claimed, and as her counsel contended in his final speech? Malaya had few white women and many men, he said, and there were times when "a woman must act to protect herself."

Seeking a verdict of justifiable homicide, the defence

counsel went on to ask the court to find that Ethel Proudlock was justified in "crushing and absolutely extinguishing...that abominable outrage" on herself if it was believed that Steward committed it.

"The man who makes such an attack on a woman is a brute beast," the counsel concluded. "One should no more hesitate to kill such a noxious animal than one should a snake."

Ethel appeared composed and confident right up to the verdict. Then she learned that the jury did not accept that William Steward was a would-be rapist, and she was found guilty of murder. She was sentenced to death, and when the judge said, "I sentence the accused to hang by the neck till she be dead" she lost her self-control and was assisted from the dock in a state of near-collapse.

Yet she still had many supporters and sympathisers. The Malaysian newspaper *Straits Budget* commented that she "should be honoured by her own sex and respected by all men who have a spark of real chivalry in their natures."

There was no evidence that Steward had been drunk, but the *Budget* thundered: "We hold quite candidly that if a man befuddles himself with liquor or becomes a murderous fiend in consequence of excess, he must be answerable for the consequences of all his actions."

Ethel Proudlock's "struggle", said the *Budget*, was "not for herself only but for the right of her sex to go to any extremity in defence of that which all pure-minded, delicately-nurtured women hold more sacred and more precious than life itself."

Whether or not he believed his wife's story, William Proudlock lost no time in cabling London, and asking the Secretary of State for the Colonies to seek a Royal pardon. Back came a reply advising him to address his appeal to the local potentate, the Sultan of Selangor. The King did not wish to interfere in what was a matter for the Sultan's discretion.

Queen Mary was cabled by the women of Kuala Lumpur, urging a pardon in consideration of the impending Coronation. Kuala Lumpur's principal business houses displayed petitions for their clients to sign, and the women of Penang cabled the King stating: "We believe from the evidence given in court that Mrs. Proudlock received great provocation and acted as she did only for the protection of her honour."

Funds were raised for an appeal, but from her cell Ethel wrote to her lawyer: "I wish to withdraw my appeal. I should have to wait at least a month before knowing what was going to happen to me. I do not feel able to do so. The suspense is simply awful. I am, as you are probably aware, in a condemned cell, watched night and day... I feel another month would deprive me of my reason. I have a horror, too, of appearing in court again...Though conscious of my own innocence of the terrible charge against me, I shrink from being stared at and pointed out as a condemned criminal..."

The Sultan did not heed the advice of British officials who wanted the death sentence to be commuted to life imprisonment in order to demonstrate the impartiality of colonial justice. He was more receptive to a petition signed by 356 "leading Chinese gentlemen of Kuala Lumpur" who urged a free pardon. In July he granted that pardon on the grounds that Mrs. Proudlock was a young mother, and on the condition that she leave the country upon her release from jail.

Ten years later Somerset Maugham visited Kuala Lumpur, heard the story of Ethel Proudlock, and wrote *The Letter*, which made its first appearance in a magazine. The heroine's name was Leslie Crosbie, but there was no doubting that she was Ethel Proudlock in a work of fiction.

Maugham stuck to the facts but changed the outcome. His instinct for the dramatic proved more than justified. In 1927 he turned the story into a play which ran for 338 performances, with Gladys Cooper in the role of Leslie Crosbie.

The play was followed by a silent movie, and then in

1940 *The Letter* was filmed again as a talkie with Bette Davis as the star.

Ethel Proudlock, meanwhile, vanished into obscurity, possibly unaware that a best-selling author was making a fortune out of her personal tragedy.

What happened to her? According to Maugham's biographer, Ted Morgan, she went to England alone and died in an asylum, deranged by the ordeal of spending a month in the condemned cell. But Eric Lawlor, the author of a recently published study of the case, *Murder on the Verandah* (Harper Collins), has dug deeper. He finds that after going to England the Proudlocks moved on to Canada in 1913. Then in 1916 Ethel Proudlock left her husband and daughter and moved to the United States, dying in Florida in 1971 at the age of 83.

Somerset Maugham's story, however, has a happier ending. To applause from the court's public gallery, Leslie Crosbie is congratulated by the judge: the verdict is "justifiable homicide."

There was a happy ending too for another woman: the wife of the lawyer who told Maugham about the case. She was celebrated for her cocktails, and known as the "Gin Queen of Singapore", and Maugham stayed with the couple in 1922. When *The Letter* was turned into a play he sent her a copy inscribed, "Here is the play which I owe so much to you." But his real debt was to neither Mrs. Dickinson nor her husband. It was to Ethel Proudlock. She could doubtless have done with the money Maugham made from her misfortune.

19

WILLIAM WILBERFORCE

Murders that inflamed a reformer's zeal

Few ships that have sailed under the British flag could ever have been as notorious as the quaintly named slave ship *Zong*.

The *Zong* left the West Coast of Africa in January, 1771, bound for Kingston, Jamaica, with a cargo of 470 slaves freshly plucked from their villages, shackled, and crammed below decks. Halfway across the Atlantic the human cargo, unused to such terrifying conditions, was swept by an epidemic.

Told of what was happening in the hold, the captain considered the matter. His insurance covered him only for those slaves lost at sea. The insurance company would reimburse him for them at a fixed price per head – but they would not pay out for any found dead on arrival at Kingston.

The captain's only concern was for keeping his ship profitable. He hadn't the slightest interest in the health of his cargo and assumed that many if not all the slaves would die anyway.

Ordering the crew to bring the shackled slaves on to the main deck, the captain had 133 of them thrown alive into the sea, many still in chains. This meant that the insurers would pay for them. When his first mate, overwhelmed by the horror of this mid-Atlantic murder scene, protested, the captain told him that dumping the slaves alive in the ocean was doing them a kindness – it would spare them a painful and lingering death from the effects of the epidemic.

Back in England the captain was charged with murder, but quickly acquitted, the court reasoning that he had done the best job he could have done in the circumstances. Then he claimed £3,960 compensation from the insurers for loss of goods and chattels.

Few people in Britain at the end of the eighteenth century saw much wrong with this chain of events. For most of them regarded slaves not as people but as property. Property did not have feelings; it could be dumped at sea if that was expedient and its loss was not a subject for grief but for an insurance pay-off.

But one Victorian was incensed by it all. He was the MP for Hull, William Wilberforce, and as every schoolboy knows it was as a result of his zealous campaigning that Parliament abolished the slave trade in 1807, and slavery in 1834. What is not so well known is that between Wilberforce's first cry against slavery and its abolition nearly half a century went by.

Despite incidents like that on the *Zong* slave ship, the truth was that countless Britons were doing very nicely out of slavery. Whole cities were prospering from it, and their ports – particularly those of London, Liverpool, Bristol and Cardiff – fairly bustled at getting rich with it. Stately homes were financed and kept going by the slave trade. When Wilberforce supporter told an audience at a Liverpool meeting that there wasn't a brick in that city that had not been cemented by the blood of a black man he was over-stating, but his metaphor had more than a grain of truth in it.

Wilberforce was the archetype Victorian gentleman – he might have been the model for Charles Smithson, the hero of *The French Lieutenant's Woman*. He was Cambridge educated, rich – he inherited a fortune from his father, a merchant in the Baltic shipping trade – a member of London's most elite clubs, a gambler, tall, urbane, witty, and consummately charming.

He spent £9,000, a huge sum in 1780, on his first and successful parliamentary election campaign. He became a great friend of William Pitt, the Prime Minister, and they travelled abroad together. But he was not travelling with Pitt when, in Nice in 1784, he read a religious book which resulted in his conversion to evangelical Christianity.

Back in London he used his parliamentary status to pursue good causes with zeal. He introduced a bill to reform criminal law. The Lords rejected it, but complimented its sponsor on his benevolent intentions. Then he procured a royal proclamation against vice and founded a society, known as the Proclamation Society, to give it teeth. The new body took a major part in prosecuting blasphemous and indecent publications.

Wilberforce wasn't the first distinguished man to tackle the slavery question. There was already a committee intent on its abolition. But sitting under an oak tree in Holwood Park, Pitt's summer residence at Keston in Kent, he made up his mind that this would be his big cause in life.

Backed by Pitt in the House of Commons, he spoke for three and a half hours, moving twelve resolutions against the slave trade. He was well supported, but the planters got the matter postponed. Undeterred, he brought in a Bill for the abolition of the slave trade. It was defeated by 163 to 88.

Wilberforce continued to hammer away in Parliament, bringing in all sorts of Bills which, although defeated, showed that the tide was gradually turning. One reason why the abolitionists did not get sufficient support was that slavery was out of sight, and therefore out of mind. It was something that happened in faraway places. Slaves were seldom seen in Britain, their exploiters operating what was known as a triangular trade. The slave ships sailed from Britain to West Africa, picked up their human cargo, took it to the Caribbean and the American colonies, and returned to England laden with cash and sugar. This system maximised the use of trading ships, and its cost in human misery was never witnessed by the people back home.

As far as the shippers were concerned, it was just too bad that around 10 per cent of a shipment of slaves failed to survive the voyage, and that on a bad trip the death toll could be as high as 30 per cent. As for the inhuman way the slaves were treated on the plantations, that too was none of the shippers' business. Who could complain when fortunes were being made out of those plantations, and when the slave-owners' profits were being invested back in Britain to boost the national economy?

This tightly-knit economic integration explains why it took Wilberforce and his supporters many years to prick the national conscience, and why they had to move cautiously, step by step, to achieve the reforms they eventually won. Throughout the early years of the nineteenth century they plugged away at the opposition. In 1807 Wilberforce's Bill for abolition of the trade was carried through two readings in the Lords. It was referred to the Commons on February 10th, 1807, debated, and voted upon. Wilberforce was too overcome with emotion to notice the cheers that greeted him when the motion was carried by 283 votes to 16.

Accomplishing the trade's abolition did not do away with slavery itself, but it was a start. The slaves themselves played a major part in what happened next. They turned to rebellion. As long ago as 1752 they had shown they could fight their way to freedom, given half a chance. There were 400 of them on the Bristol slave ship *Marlborough*, which had a crew of 35 . One day at sea, while most of the sailors were below, 28 of the slaves on deck managed to seize muskets, kill 27 of her crew, take over the ship and sail her back to Africa.

Their story had a less than happy ending when they fell out among themselves. They were from two different regions and by the time they made landfall 100 ex-slaves lay dead. The survivors, however, reached their homes safely, having shown that slaves could be a force to be reckoned with.

Eight years later, slaves made a less successful bid to escape from the slave ship *Robert* while it was lying off shore. They killed two members of the crew who were asleep, but were then overpowered. They were tortured, and some were made to eat each other.

Periodically slave rebellions broke out in the plantations, triggered by inhuman conditions. The most dramatic of these occurred in Jamaica in 1831, long after the slave trade was abolished but three years before slaves were finally given their freedom. The uprising became known as Sam Sharpe's Revolt, because it was believed to have been encouraged by Sharpe, an itinerant black Baptist deacon. He was said to have urged his congregations to stop work on Christmas Day in an attempt to achieve freedom from their bondage.

This was intended to be a peaceful withdrawal of labour. It got out of hand when rumours spread that emancipation had already been granted, and the news was being deliberately kept from the slaves by their masters.

Some of the slaves armed themselves, forming a small army. By the time militiamen had put down their revolt a fortnight later, more than 200 slaves had been killed, 14 whites were dead, and property worth more than £1 million had been destroyed. In retribution, the authorities executed a further 312 rebellious slaves to teach the rest a lesson.

A more modest revolt was put down even more savagely 15 years earlier. This was led by a slave named Bussa who had been promoted to manage the workers on a plantation in Barbados. Only one black and one white were killed in the uprising, but in reprisal women and children were murdered indiscriminately, mostly by trigger-happy plantation owners and other settlers who formed the militia. One hundred and forty-four slaves were executed, and a further 120 died from wounds received in the rebellion.

By the time of Sam Sharpe's Revolt plantation owners were already easing their workers' conditions with various safety-valve privileges intended to prevent the pot from boiling over. Slaves were now allowed to marry and raise families, attend church services and travel from one plantation to another. These improvements, however, made them aware of how much more they were missing, and gave rise to demands for further concessions.

When it became clear that Britain was not prepared to provide enough troops to keep dissident slaves down indefinitely, the plantation owners had to recognise that sooner or later the slaves would have to be given their freedom. This meant among other things that their masters would no longer be able to force slave-girls to have sex with them, a practice which over the years had produced many half-caste children.

Thomas Thistlewood, a slave-owner in the Caribbean, took as his principal mistress his own slave housekeeper, but he did not stop at her. Every year he noted in his diary how he had celebrated his birthday by raping a virgin. His journal notes when and where he sexually abused other slave-women on his plantations. Sometimes he raped them in the sugar cane fields; on other occasions he dragged them first to one of his many houses.

William Wilberforce did not live to see the abolition of slavery which put an end to the liberties of Thistlewood and his kind. Ill-health compelled him to retire from Parliament in 1825, and he died in 1833, the year the Abolition of Slavery Act was passed, to be implemented a year later.

Even under this Act the freed slaves were not to enjoy their independence without strings. If they attempted to leave their plantations they would be prosecuted as vagrants, and they were prohibited from owning any plot of land amounting to more than a small garden. In addition, they were not to leave their employers for six years with effect from the Act coming into force. This period, ironically termed their "apprenticeship," entailed working a 10-hour day for about sixpence (two and a half new pence) a day, and from that sum rent was deducted. Absenteeism was punished by imprisonment. Recalcitrant ex-slaves of both sexes could be flogged.

According to those who drew up the Act, the purpose of these harsh regulations for those who were now supposed to be at liberty was to "protect" the freed slaves from "living in idleness to the detriment of the state." The Colonial Office loftily opined: "A state of things where the Negro escaped the necessity of labour would be as bad for him as for his owner. He would be cut off from civilising influences, would have no incentive to better his condition or to impose any but the slightest degree of discipline on himself. Thus he might well become a more degraded being than his ancestors in Africa."

A blind eye was turned to the "civilising influence" of slave owners like Thomas Thistlewood, dedicated to degrading his workers even further. And when abolition became law the slave owners were handed a sweetener in the form of compensation totalling nearly £20 million. No one thought of compensating the freed slaves for their years of lost liberty and unpaid labour.

If anyone hoped that the former slave owners might use some of their compensation altruistically they were disappointed. Instead of spending their windfalls on improving the local colonial economy, they invested in property and bonds in Britain.

When the great dream of freeing the slaves was finally realised things took a wrong turn. Sugar production slumped, and half of Jamaica's plantations went bankrupt. In British Guiana and Trinidad the former slaves demonstrated their new independence by staging strikes. The result was that many of them lost their jobs, for the planters responded by importing indentured workers from India.

In the immediate aftermath of the abolition of slavery the successful campaign of Wilberforce and his supporters seemed to many to have been a foreseeable disaster. What little thought was devoted to the slaves' transition from bondage to independence was inspired by self-interest – the needs of the whites, not those of the blacks. In time of course the former slaves sorted things out for themselves. They learned trades, became shopkeepers, acquired education, joined the professions. In the long run Wilberforce would have been proud of his achievement. But in the short run he would have been dismayed.

20

THE BASKERVILLES:

Was this the real-life killer hound?

Sir Arthur Conan Doyle, as the celebrated creator of Sherlock Holmes eventually became, was on a golfing holiday in Cromer, Norfolk, in 1901, when he was told an enthralling story by Fletcher Robinson, a *Daily Express* journalist who he had earlier met on a trip to South Africa.

Robinson had heard the tale from the novelist and writer Max Pemberton, and he passed it on to Conan Doyle as an example of West Country folk-lore.

It recounted how many centuries ago one of the squires of Dartmoor, one Richard Cabell of Brook Manor, murdered his wife. Her dog, a large and fearsome animal, then turned on the murderous husband and killed him, but not before the dying Cabell had fatally stabbed the dog with the same knife with which he had killed his wife.

Ever since that day Cabell's descendants were plagued by a savage spectral hound.

One of these Cabells, apparently as lawless as Richard the murderer, abducted a young girl on the moor and took her prisoner to his manor. But while Cabell caroused with his friends, the girl escaped.

In his fury at discovering her gone, the squire announced a Faustian pact – the devil could have his body and soul if only he could catch her. Then, giving the hounds the scent of her handkerchief, he set off across the moor in pursuit, his friends trailing behind him.

In a short while they lost sight of Cabell and were startled to see his horse, riderless, suddenly emerge from the mist. Where, they wondered, was the squire ...?

As Fletcher Robinson finished telling the story to Conan Doyle the author's eyes lit up. For the rest of that day he couldn't stop thinking about it. The more he pondered, the more the legend appealed to him as material for a case for his celebrated detective.

That evening Conan Doyle discussed it further with Fletcher Robinson, and the two men talked of collaborating to write the story. They went together to Dartmoor to research the area and to absorb "local colour," staying at Rowe's Duchy Hotel at Princetown and visiting Brook Manor.

Full of enthusiasm Conan Doyle wrote to tell his mother of the project, saying the story would be "a real creeper!"

Conan Doyle began to expand the legend, and to bring in other material which he discovered along the way. And thus was born one of the greatest of all the Sherlock Holmes stories – *The Hound of the Baskervilles.*

The author rejected the name Cabell because he didn't think it had the right ring about it, and opted for Baskerville. So it was that in *The Hound of the Baskervilles*, when Hugo Baskerville's friends, like Cabell's friends, saw the riderless horse coming out of the mist they too wondered what had happened to the squire.

They soon found out. Catching up with the hounds, they found them peering into a narrow valley and whimpering with fear. Three of Baskerville's friends rode forward to investigate – and saw something that made their hair stand on end.

"Standing over Hugo, and plucking at his throat, there stood a foul thing, a great black beast shaped like a hound, yet larger than any hound that ever mortal eyes had rested upon. And even as they looked the thing tore the throat out of Hugo Baskerville..."

Then, "as it turned its blazing eyes and dripping jaws upon them, the three shrieked with fear and rode for dear life, still screaming, across the moor ..."

And since that time the Baskervilles, like the Cabells, were plagued by the hound, many of them dying bloody, mysterious deaths.

This was the Curse of the Baskervilles, and it seemed to strike again centuries later when Sherlock Holmes was called in to investigate in Conan Doyle's dramatic story.

While Conan Doyle was working on his tale another haunted family are believed to have come into the picture. These were the Vaughans, of Hergest Court, Hereford and Worcester, who, according to local folk-lore, were plagued by a savage animal known as the Black Dog of Hergest. Significantly, the Vaughans were related to the Baskervilles of Clyro Court, Hay-on-Wye. Lady Dorothy Baskerville is said to have consented to the author using her family's name – Conan Doyle also thought that Vaughan did not have the right ring to it.

Another account, however, has it that Conan Doyle took the name from Henry Baskerville, a coachman who drove him around Devon while he researched the novel's setting.

It was initially agreed that *The Hound of the Baskervilles* should be published under the names of Conan Doyle and Fletcher Robinson, as joint authors, and Robinson later told friends that Doyle had paid him to write the first instalment of the story for a magazine. This claim, though, hardly bears scrutiny. The opening chapters of the novel are pure Conan Doyle, his style evident in every line.

But not wishing to take all the credit, Conan Doyle acknowledged his debt to Fletcher Robinson in a short note prefacing the book when it was published in 1902: "My dear Robinson, it was to your account of a West Country legend that this tales owes its inception. For this and for your help in the details all thanks. Yours most truly, A. Conan Doyle."

Robinson realised that his friend was on to a big money-spender with his creation of Sherlock Holmes, so he thought up a detective of his own, named Addington Peace, whose exploits Robinson chronicled in *Lady's*

Home Magazine. The publicity for Addington Peace described him as "the greatest detective who ever lived," and it also described Fletcher Robinson as "the collaborator with Sir A. Conan Doyle in *The Hound of the Baskervilles*." That was stretching a point, of course, but today no one remembers Addington Peace, while Sherlock Holmes is still as large as life.

In creating his fearsome hound, Conan Doyle had no shortage of models to choose from. Many other regions in Britain have their own stories of savage ghostly animals – they include the Black Shuck of East Anglia and the Black Dog of Lyme Regis. And Yorkshire folk still firmly believe that the hound of the Baskervilles was based on the legend of the Barguest, a monstrous dog which hunted solitary wayfarers at night. The legend says that the traveller's only escape from this terrifying animal was to cross the gorge of Trollers Gill – a tributary of the River Wharfe, near Ilkley – for the Barguest feared water.

Most likely Conan Doyle was aware of the Barguest because he spent his schooldays at Stonyhurst in Lancashire, not far from the Yorkshire border. But there is no doubt that the story of the Cabells of Brook Manor was his principal inspiration, helped along by the attraction of Dartmoor as a suitably forbidding setting, with its bogs, its bleakness and the added drama of escaped convicts.

Dr. Watson, Holmes's friend, describes their arrival there in suitably sombre terms: "There rose in the distance a grey, melancholy hill with a strange jagged summit, dim and vague in the distance, like some fantastic landscape in a dream ... our wagonette had topped a rise and in front of us rose the huge expanse of the moor, mottled with gnarled and craggy cairns and tors ... Suddenly we looked down into a cup-like depression patched with stunted oaks and firs which had been twisted by the fury of years of storm."

This was a fitting place to be roamed by a larger-than-life hound, its jaws slavering. Curiously, in our own times Dartmoor has become the haunt of another "monster," a creature said to be bigger than a hound and believed to be an escaped black puma. Sightings have been reported periodically, but the animal seems to be as elusive as the spectral dogs of folk-lore and all attempts to trap it have come to nothing.

Unfortunately, Sherlock Holmes isn't around now. He would have known what to do.